D0735635

SEMIOTEXT(E) INTERVENTION SERIES

© La Fabrique Éditions, 2016.

Published by Semiotext(e)
PO BOX 629, South Pasadena, CA 91031
www.semiotexte.com

Thanks to John Ebert, Janique Vigier, and Noura Wedell.

Inside cover photograph: Hassane Mezine
Design: Hedi El Kholti

ISBN: 978-1-63590-003-3
Distributed by The MIT Press, Cambridge, Mass.
and London, England
Printed in the United States of America

Houria Bouteldja

Whites, Jews, and Us

Toward a Politics of Revolutionary Love

Foreword by Cornel West

Translated by Rachel Valinsky

semiotext(e)
intervention
series □ 22

Contents

Foreword by Cornel West

THE END OF IMPERIAL INNOCENCE

This book is a courageous and controversial act of revolutionary love. Houria Bouteldja's bold and critical challenge to all of us—especially those who claim to be leftists or progressives—builds on the rich legacies of Malcolm X, Jean Genet, Aimé Césaire, Audre Lorde, James Baldwin, Frantz Fanon, and Chela Sandoval. This challenge consists of a powerful intellectual case against imperial innocence and a poignant cry of the heart for an indigenous revolutionary politics—a politics that is unapologetically anti-patriarchal, anti-capitalist, and anti-imperialist grounded in the doings and sufferings of colonized peoples. It comes as no surprise that our present moment of escalating neo-fascist regimes, tightening patriarchal practices and neoliberal free-market ideologies have thrown the left and progressive voices into a panic. And such a panic makes it difficult to have a robust and painful dialogue about whiteness, Zionism, patriarchy, and empire.

Does not the end of imperial innocence entail the rejection of social democracy or neoliberal politics—with their attendant "white good conscience," top-down feminism, bourgeois multiculturalism, and refusal to target a vicious Israeli occupation of Palestinian lands and people? Do not the precious lives of hundreds of thousands of Muslims killed by US and NATO Armed Forces (including immoral drone strikes) have any moral weight in how we understand the ugly forms of xenophobia spilling out of control in the US and Europe? What does a candid and compassionate indictment of Zionist practices on the West Bank and Gaza look like that avoids anti-Jewish hatred and contempt? How does a "decolonizing internationalism" proceed in the face of entrenched nationalisms or neoliberal cosmopolitanism? Can a "decolonial feminism"—with its echoes from the work of the visionary bell hooks in the very belly of the US imperial beast—lead toward a "concrete emancipation" that resists patriarchal religions and elite feminisms? As the "genocides, ecodisasters, and ethnocides" continue to surface, "wedded to new secular hierarchies," either a new "great We of a decolonized majority" rooted in visions beyond empire, capitalism, whiteness, and patriarchy and grounded in a revolutionary love can guide us or we all succumb to the "ancient forces of human greed and violence." These questions and issues demand the best of who we are—and none of us have a monopoly on the truth and justice they require and solicit. There is a genuine humility in this book—and its sense of urgency and dire emergency behooves us to wrestle with its rich contents.

To béba, from the top of his crane.

Blessed are the cracked, for they shall let in the light.

I would like to thank the three mad ones God had the kindness to place on my path and without whom this book would never have existed. By "mad" I mean radical activists who act on their ideals without thinking too much about the consequences of their actions, who take risks without worrying too much about their immediate interests, and who make life lighter because when you're with them, to be an activist is also to laugh. Those who have been lucky enough to meet them know what I mean.

I am thinking first of Youssef Boussoumah, a tireless militant for the Palestinian cause, who patiently corrected my lack of political knowledge; of my brother Ramon Grosfoguel a professor at UC Berkeley, for his faith, his unshakable commitment, and his profound friendship; and finally, of Sadri Khiari, my alter ego, to whom I feel I owe something essential. If I had not, for obvious reasons, dedicated this book to my father, it is to him that I would have paid this homage.

My deepest gratitude also goes to all the activists of the PIR, to those who have recently joined us and to those who were with us from the very beginning, and especially to Mehdi Meftah, Hassan Mezine, M'baïreh Lisette, Nadia Tengout, and Atman Zerkaoui. Apologies to all those whom I have not mentioned. My gratitude goes to all the activists in the Euro-American decolonial network on which much of my hope is based, and especially Marta Araujo, Paola Bacchetta, Hatem Bazian, Claire Grosfoguel, Sandew Hira, Nelson Maldonaldo Torrès, Arzu Merali, Andrea Meza, Kwamé Nimako, Nordine Saidi, Salman Sayyid, Boaventura de Suza Santos, and Silvia Rodriguez Maeso.

I would also like to thank my brothers, sisters, and friends, fellow travelers who have crossed paths with the Indigenous and who I feel are equally responsible for this book. I am thinking about the entire galaxy of "Islamo-Leftists" and anticolonialists I know. There are too few of them to really have any weight in the political balance of power but too many of them to be named here. I am thinking in particular of Hamid Amara, Omar Benderra, Hassan Benghabrit, Henri

Braun, Walid Charara, Raphaël Confiant, Christine Delphy, Mireille Fanon Mendès-France, Alain Gresh, Laurent Lévy, Franco Lollia, Gus Massiah, Vanessa Thompson, Saidou Zepetista, Joby Valente.... The others will probably recognize themselves.

Big thanks to René Monzat, Saadane Sadgui, Christophe Montaucieux, and Félix Boggio Ewanjé-Epée for their attentive reading, their informed recommendations, and their friendship.

How could I neglect to express my profound respect to my French editors? First, to Eric Hazan, for his enthusiasm and his precious and generous confidence, and also to Stella Magliani-Belkacem for her professionalism, her friendship, and her great devotion. To both of them for having tirelessly supported me despite the heavy outcry provoked by the book. To my American editors, Sylvère Lotringer and Hedi El Kholti, for the time and interest which they gave to my work and the confidence which I was accorded. My deepest acknowledgement goes out to my translator Rachel Valinsky, and to the great Cornel West who has done me the honor of writing the foreword.

A final, friendly salute to all the immigration activists, past and present, and in particular, to Ali el Baz and Saad Abssi, but also to those I have known who are no longer with us. I am thinking about

Mouloud Aounit and Hamida Ben Sadia. And since we must salute the dead, a final homage shall go to Larbi Ben M'hidi, for whom I have a profound admiration, and to Fernand Iveton, whose sacrifice will never cease to move and shake me. Right before being guillotined, he declared: "A man's life, my life, matters little. What matters is Algeria, its future. And Algeria will be free tomorrow. I am convinced that the friendship between the French and the Algerians will one day be mended." He was far off the mark and my sorrow is all the greater for it. May they rest in peace.

A few remarks on what follows: I draw my hope and sensibility from history and from the contemporary state of North African and Arab-Berber-Muslim immigration. I speak from this perspective. Moreover, I borrow the phrase "revolutionary love" from Chela Sandoval, a Chicana activist who was the first person, to my knowledge, to use it. I don't know what meaning she attributed to it but I liked the expression. Finally, the categories I use: "Whites," "Jews," "Indigenous women," and "Indigenous" are social and political. They are the product of modern history in the same way terms like "workers" or "women" are. In no way do they bear on the subjectivity or biological determinism of individuals. Rather, they speak to their condition and status.

1

SHOOT SARTRE!

"Shoot Sartre!" The French philosopher takes a stand in favor of Algeria's independence. He comes under fire from thousands of veterans on the Champs-Élysées on October 3rd, 1960. Sartre is not Camus. Sartre's first revolt, he confessed, was to discover at the age of fourteen that the colonies were a "seizure on the part of the state" and a "totally discreditable [action]." To which he added: "The freedom that made me a man made colonialism something abject."[1] As far as colonialism and racism are concerned, true to his adolescent conscience, he would almost never go wrong. He would mobilize against the "cancer" that is apartheid, against the United States' segregationist regime; he would support the Cuban and Viêt Minh revolutions. He would even declare himself a suitcase carrier[2] for the FLN.[3] No, he is decidedly not Camus, against whom the Algerian poet Kateb Yacine would pronounce a relentless indictment.

"Killing a European is killing two birds with one stone, eliminating in one go oppressor and oppressed: leaving one man dead and the other free."[4] Sartre never claimed to be a pacifist. He demonstrated this once again in 1972 during the Olympic Games in Munich. In accordance with his commitments in Algeria, he regarded terrorism as "a terrible weapon," to be sure, but argued that the oppressed have no other recourse. For him, the Black September attacks, which claimed the lives of eleven Israeli teammates, "succeeded perfectly," given that the Palestinian question had finally been presented to millions of television viewers across the world, "more tragically than at the UN where the Palestinians are not represented."[5]

Sartre's blood was shed. I find it easy to imagine Sartre's devastation when he took a stand in favor of Black September. He mutilated his soul. But this was not the fatal blow. Sartre survived. For indeed, the man who wrote the preface to *The Wretched of the Earth* had not yet completed his task: to kill the white man. Sartre is not Camus, but he is not Genet, either. For, beyond his empathy for the colonized and their legitimate use of violence, for him, nothing can dethrone the legitimate existence of Israel.

In 1948, he took a stand for the creation of the Jewish state and defended Zionist peace, for "an independent, free, and peaceful state."[6] Following in Simone de Beauvoir's footsteps, he supported Jewish immigration to Palestine.[7] "The Jews must be armed: this is the UN's most immediate task," he declared. We cannot turn away from the Jewish cause, unless we also accept our treatment as murderers.[8] And he continued: "There is no Jewish problem. It is an international problem. It is the responsibility of the Aryans to help the Jews. The problem involves all of humanity. Indeed, it's a human problem."[9] In 1949, he would say: "We must rejoice that an autonomous Israeli state has legitimated the hopes and combats of Jews throughout the world.... The formation of the Palestinian state[10] must be considered one of the most important events of our era, one of the few that allows us today to preserve hope."[11]

Whose hope?

He who declared "It is the anti-Semite who *makes* the Jew" now prolonged the anti-Semitic project in its Zionist form and participated in the construction of the greatest prison for Jews.[12] In a rush to bury Auschwitz and to save the white man's soul, he dug the Jew's grave. The Palestinian was there, just by chance. He crushed him. Sartre's good white conscience... It is this conscience that prevents him from completing his task: to liquidate the white man. In order to exterminate the white man who tormented him, he would have had to have written: "Killing an Israeli is killing two birds with one stone, eliminating in one go oppressor and oppressed: leaving one dead man and the other free." To resign himself to the oppressor's defeat or death, even if he were Jewish. This is the step Sartre did not know how to take. This is his failure. The white man resisted. Is Philo-Semitism not the last refuge of white humanism?

In his editorial in *Les Temps Modernes* dedicated to the Israeli-Palestinian "conflict" published a few days before the war in 1967, Sartre sticks to his guns.[13] Though he's upset by Israel's excesses, his fidelity to the Zionist project remained intact. Josie Fanon, Frantz Fanon's widow, would reproach him for having become associated with the "hysterical clamoring of the French 'Left'" and would ask François Maspero to remove Sartre's preface to *The Wretched of the Earth* from future editions. "There is no longer anything in common between Sartre and us, between Sartre and Fanon. Sartre who, in 1961, dreamt of joining those who make human history has passed into the other camp. The camp of the assassin. The camp of those who kill in Vietnam, in the Middle East, in Africa, in Latin America."[14] No, Sartre is not Genet. And Josie Fanon knew this.

In 1975, did he not protest, along with Mitterand, Mendès France, and Malraux—an admirable bunch—against the UN resolution that rightly assimilated Zionism with racism?[15]

Fucking Arabs! Their stubbornness in denying the existence of Israel delays the "evolution of the Middle East toward socialism..." and postpones the prospect of peace, which would alleviate the Sartrian spleen and its bad conscience. In 1976, his wish was granted. The Egyptian president Sadat would visit the Memorial to the Martyrs of the Deportation. The same year, he received the title of doctor *honoris causa* from the University of Jerusalem at the Israeli embassy. Sartre would die an anticolonialist and a Zionist. He would die white. This would not be the least of his paradoxes.

In this way, he stands as an allegory of the post-war French Left.

Sartre does not belong to the wave of "new philosophers" and cannot, in all decency, be held accountable for the advent of social democracy and its cardinal mission: to bury socialism in order to save capitalism. If the current Left's actions reflected its commitments, we would be all the better for it. However, we have reason to believe that the Left's whiteness has affected its constitution.

Sartre did not know how to radically betray his race. He did not know how to be Genet... who rejoiced at France's defeat to the Germans in 1940, and later on in Saigon and Algeria. He rejoiced at France's thrashing in Dien Bien Phu. Because, you see, occupied France was also colonial France. Was it not? Wasn't the France of the French Resistance also the same France that would go and spread terror in Sétif and Guelma on a certain 8th of May, 1945, and then in Madagascar, and in Cameroon? "The debacle of the French army was also that of the great military corps who condemned Dreyfus, wasn't it?"[16] For, to be sure, there is class conflict, but there is also racial conflict.

What I like about Genet is that he couldn't care less about Hitler. And paradoxically, in my eyes, he succeeded in being a radical friend to the two great historical victims of the white order: the Jews and the colonized. There is no trace of philanthropy in him, either in favor of the Jews, the Black Panthers, or the Palestinians. Rather, there is a deaf anger against the injustice that was done to them by his own race. Didn't he welcome the suppression of the death penalty in France with cynical indifference, while propriety called for sanctimonious emotions and celebrated this new step toward civilization? Genet's position falls like a guillotine on the white man's head: "As long as France does not engage in what has been called North-South politics, as long as it is not more concerned with immigrant workers or the former colonies, French politics doesn't interest me at all. Whether or not white men's heads get cut off or not doesn't particularly interest me." Because "creating a democracy in the country that used to be called the 'metropole' in relation to its colonies, is still to be creating a democracy that works against black countries, Arab countries, and others...."[17] There is something like an aesthetics in this indifference toward Hitler. It is visionary. Was it necessary to be a poet to achieve this grace? The main political groups' compulsive eagerness to turn the Nazi leader into an accident of European history, and to reduce Vichy and all forms of collaboration to simple interlude, could not fool "the angel of Reims."[18] I used the term "indifference." Not empathy, not collusion. Could he revile Hitler and spare France, which had shown itself "rotten [in its] treatment of people in Indochina and Algeria, in Madagascar"? "Intoxicating" is how he described his feeling toward the French defeat against Hitler.[19] How could one cheerfully rejoice at the end of Nazism all the while accommodating the genesis of colonialism and the pursuit of the imperialist project by other means? Could one recklessly isolate the Nazi moment from all other Western crimes and genocides? Did one have the moral right to take the Germans to task while offloading the French, the British, and the Americans? This brings to mind Césaire's, for whom "Nazism [was] a form of colonization of the white man by the white man, a 'shock in return' to the European colonizers"[20]: "A civilization which justifies colonization…calls for its Hitler, I mean its punishment."[21] Indeed, Hitler, writes Césaire, "applied to Europe colonialist procedures which until then had been reserved exclusively for the Arabs of Algeria, the coolies of India, and the blacks of Africa."[22]

Another thing I like about Genet is that he doesn't have any kind of obsequious feeling toward us. But he knows how to discern the invisible proposition made to white people by radical activists of the black cause, the Palestinian cause, and the Third World cause. He knows that any indigenous person who rises up against the white man grants him, in the same movement, the chance to save himself. He intimates that behind Malcom X's radical resistance is his own salvation. Genet knows this, and every time an indigenous person gave him this opportunity, he took it. This is why Malcom X loved Genet from beyond the grave. It is only between these two men that the word "peace" has a meaning. It has a meaning because it is irrigated by revolutionary love.

But Malcom X cannot love Genet without loving his own people *above all else*. It is his legacy to all of the world's non-white people. Thanks to him, I am an heiress.

First, we have to love each other…

Why am I writing this book? Probably to be forgiven for the initial cowardice of this unbearable indigenous condition of mine. That time when, as a high school student, on my way to a school trip to New York, I asked my parents who had accompanied me to the airport to stay hidden, out of sight from my teachers and classmates, because "the other parents didn't accompany their kids." A lousy fib. I was ashamed of them. They looked too poor and too much like immigrants, with their Arab faces, as they proudly watched me fly off to the country of Uncle Sam. They did not protest. They hid and I naively believed that they fell for it. What I failed to realize until this day is that they accompanied me in the lie. They even supported it without batting an eye so that I could go further than them. And, to be ashamed of yourself, for us, is like a second skin. "Arabs are the last race after toads," my father would say. A phrase he must have heard on a construction site and made his own through the conviction of the colonized. He was not about to recant at the airport. Since then, an asbestos cancer carried him away. A worker's cancer. Yes, I need to be forgiven by him.

Why am I writing this book? Because I am not innocent. I live in France. I live in the West. I am white. Nothing can absolve me of this. I hate the white good conscience. I curse it. It sits on the Right's left, at the heart of social democracy. This is where it has reigned for a long time, blooming and radiant. Today, the Right is faded, worn out.

Its old demons are catching up with it, and the masks are falling off. But it is still breathing. It hasn't succeeded in conquering my territory yet, thank God. I am not looking for an escape. Of course, the encounter with the great South terrifies me, but I surrender. I don't flee the undocumented worker's gaze and I don't avert my own from the starving Harraga who wash up on our shores, dead or alive. I would rather come clean. I am a criminal. But an extremely sophisticated one. I don't have any blood on my hands. That would be too vulgar. No justice system in the world would drag me to court. I outsource my crime. Between my crime and I, there's the bomb. I own nuclear fire. My bomb threatens all *métèques*[23] and protects my interests. Between my crime and I, first there is geographic distance and then geopolitical distance. But there are also great international bodies: the UN, the IMF, NATO, multinationals, the banking system. Between my crime and I, there are national bodies: democracy, the rule of law, the Republic, the elections. Between my crime and I, there are beautiful ideas: human rights, universalism, freedom, humanism, secularism, the memory of the Shoah, feminism, Marxism, Third Worldism. And even suitcase carriers. They stand at the pinnacle of white heroism. I respect them though. I wish I could respect them more, but they are already hostages of good conscience. The foils of the white

Left. Between my crime and I, there is the renewal and metamorphosis of great ideas, should the "beautiful soul" come to expire: fair trade, ecology, organic commerce.

Between me and my crime, there is my father's sweat and salary, social welfare, paid leave, labor law, school holidays, summer camp, hot water, heat, public transportation, my passport.... I am detached from my victim—and from my crime—by an insurmountable distance. This distance stretches. European check points have moved south. Fifty years after the independence movements, North Africa is the one subduing its own citizens and black Africans. I was going to say "my African brothers." But I no longer dare to, now that I have admitted my crime. Farewell Bandung. Sometimes the distance between my crime and I shrinks. Bombs explode in the subway. Towers are struck by airplanes and collapse like a house of cards. The journalists of a famous magazine are decimated. But immediately, good conscience does its work. "We are all American!" "We are all Charlie." This is the democrats' rallying cry. The sacred union. They are all American. They are all Charlie. They are all white.

If I were judged for my crime, I wouldn't claim my innocence. But I would plead extenuating circumstances. I am not exactly white. I am whitened. I am here because I was thrown up by

History. I am here because white people were in my country, because they are still there. What am I? An *Indigenous of the Republic*.[24] Above all, I am a victim. I have lost my humanity. In 1492 and again, in 1830.[25] And my whole life is spent recovering it. Not all time periods are equally cruel to me, but my suffering is infinite. Ever since I have seen white ferociousness beat down upon me, I have known that I would never find myself again. My integrity is lost to me and to humanity forever. I am a bastard child. I only have one conscience, which awakens my memories of 1492. A memory transmitted from generation to generation that resists the industry of lies. Thanks to this memory, I know with the assurance of my faith and with intense joy that the "Native Americans" were "the good guys." It's true; my bomb protects my indigenous aristocratic interests, but in fact, I only benefit from them accidentally. I am not their primary recipient, far from it, and my immigrant parents even less. I am in the lowest strata of the profiteers. Above me are the white profiteers. The white population that owns France: the proletarians, the civil servants, the middle classes. My oppressors. They are the small shareholders of the vast enterprise of the world's dispossession. Above them is the class of great possessors, of capitalists, of great financiers. In exchange for the complicity of the white subaltern classes, this class knew how to negotiate a greater distribution of the riches from the gigantic hold-up, as well as a—very monitored—participation in the process of political decision-making that we proudly call "democracy." My white fellow citizens believe in democracy. It's *in their best interest* to believe in it. This is why they worship it. But their conscience is crumpled. It seeks more comfort. To sleep in peace is essential. And to wake up, proud of one's own genius, is even better. Hell is other people. Humanism needed to be invented and so it was.

And the South, I know it, I'm from there. My parents transported it with them when they settled in France. They stayed there and the South took hold of me; it never left me. It settled in my head and swore to stay there forever. To torture me. All the better. Without it, I would be nothing but a social climber. The South is here and observes me with its big eyes.

Why am I writing this book?

Because I share Gramsci's anxiety:

"The old is dying and the new cannot be born; in this interregnum a great variety of morbid symptoms appear."[26] The fascist symptom, born in the entrails of Western modernity. Of course, the West is not what it used to be. China woke up. I find no reason to rejoice from this but I'm sure, however, that the decline of the squatter of

Olympus is good news for humanity. Yet, I am terribly afraid of it. The West and its habit of reaching out in times of acute crisis… How will it crush us in its convulsions? To ward off this gloomy fate, some will say that "the African man has not sufficiently entered into history,"[27] others that "all civilizations are not equal"[28] or others still will celebrate "the positive role of France's presence abroad."[29] This is the swansong. Césaire's words resonate: "A civilization which justifies colonization… calls for its Hitler… its punishment." Hence my question: what can we offer white people in exchange for their decline and for the wars that will ensue? There is only one answer: peace. There is only one way: revolutionary love. The lines that follow are but an umpteenth—probably desperate—attempt to generate this hope. In truth, only my frightening vanity allows me to believe in it. A vanity which I share with Sadri Khiari, another gentle dreamer, who made this statement: "Because it is an indispensable partner to the indigenous people, the Left is their primary opponent."[30]

We must do away with it.

"Shoot Sartre!" It's not nostalgia for a French Algeria speaking. It's me, the indigenous woman.

2

YOU, WHITE PEOPLE

MAFALDA: *"Today, I read a very depressing fact in the newspaper. 'There are 43 million children in the world who work under unacceptable conditions.' Can you believe it? This information comes from the International Labor Organization! 43 million children who must work for a living!'"*
SUZANITA: "So what? Is it out fault? No! Can we do anything about it? No! The only thing we can do is to be indignant and cry out: 'It's a scandal!!! IT'S A SCANDAL!' There, You cry it out too: It's a scandal!! That way, the case will be closed and we can play in peace."[1]

I think therefore I am. I think therefore I am… God.

Who is hiding behind this Cartesian "I"? When the formula was first pronounced, America had been "discovered" for two hundred years.

Descartes was in Amsterdam, the new center of the world system. Is it possible to extract this "I" from the political context of its enunciation? No, answers South American philosopher, Enrique Dussel. This "I" is a conquering "I." It is armed. It is empowered with fire, on the one hand, and the Bible, on the other. It is a predator. Its victories are intoxicating. We must "render ourselves, as it were, masters and possessors of nature," continues Descartes.[2] The Cartesian "I" affirms itself. It wants to defy death. It is this "I" that will from now on occupy the center. I think therefore I am the one who decides, I think therefore I am the one who dominates, I think therefore I am the one who subjugates, pillages, steals, rapes, commits genocide. I think therefore I am a modern, virile, capitalist, imperialist man. The Cartesian "I" will lay the philosophical ground for whiteness. It will secularize God's attributes and confer them to the Western God, who is, in fact, none other than a parable of the white man.

This is how you were born.

I have never been able to say "we" and include you.

You don't deserve it. And even if, to force the hand of fate, I did include you in this "we," you wouldn't recognize me within it. I am not one of you and because I am not a beggar, I will not ask you for anything. And yet, I cannot quite bring myself to exclude you. I have neither the power nor the will to do so. Exclusion is your prerogative. I am not you and refuse to become you. All I want is to escape you as much as I can.

I see you, I spend time with you, I observe you. You all wear that face of *Innocence.* This is your ultimate victory. You succeeded in exonerating yourselves. And this victory becomes sublime when you see us questioning ourselves and our brothers about our own guilt. "If we are colonized, it is because we are colonizable."[3] We are guilty; you are *innocent.* And you have made us guardians of your innocence. This innocence strikes me. A newborn is less innocent—and may even, at times, appear more vicious. You have made yourselves into angels. Angels freed from all earthly justice. You turn your victims into persecutors and impunity into your kingdom. You are angels because you have the power to declare yourselves angels and us barbarians.

> Angel of kindness, have you tasted hate?
> With hands clenched in the dark, and tears
>   of gall,
> When Vengeance beats her hellish battle-call,
> And makes herself the captain of our fate,
> Angel of kindness, have you tasted hate?[4]

On August 8, 1945, *Le Monde*'s headlines read: "A scientific revolution: Americans launch their first atomic bomb on Japan." Angels wrote these lines.

Fifty-six years later, on September 11th, 2001, these same angels cried: "We are all American." We are all American…. We are all white. White as snow; white as the color of Innocence. Innocents. The culprits will recognize themselves. Yasser Arafat, the Palestinian leader, recognized himself and immediately donated his blood to the innocents of September 11th. He gave them the blood of the Palestinians, my blood, and Geronimo's. As I write these lines, I am in Australia. With an authentic *innocent* population. According to the numbers, Australia has one of the highest indices of human development in the world. It's good to live here. The Aboriginals were exterminated. Those that remain are homeless and drown their guilt in alcohol. Until recently, they were not even included in the census, as they were considered part of the fauna. Their life expectancy is 46 years; the national median is 78. In the street, they don't look at me. They walk on like ghosts. They are in a parallel world. The world of the barbarians. Since I am a bit of one too, I see them. What to do? Nothing. It's too late.

Sometimes, things happen.

"There are no homosexuals in Iran." It's Ahmadinejad speaking. This retort pierced through my skull. I frame it, admire it. "There are no homosexuals in Iran." I am petrified. There are people who stand fascinated in front of a work of art for a long time. This had the same effect on me. Ahmadinejad, my hero. The world can't get over it. Western media, observers, Americans, Europeans, the Left, the Right, men, women, gays. Civilization is indignant. "There are no homosexuals in Iran." These words are painful. But they are violent and of exquisite bad faith. To appreciate them, you have to be a bit of a shoe-thrower. A pathetic emotion, I must admit.

Let's admire the scene. Nothing could be more sublime. It takes place in 2008 in the United States at Columbia University in New York, the famous leftist university. Ahmadinejad is traveling on official business and is set to deliver a speech at the UN, just as Abu Ghraib is raging at the heart of every polemic.

The voice: "Iran lynches homosexuals on the public square."

Ahmadinejad: "There are no homosexuals in Iran." Astonishment. General outcry. Or almost. At least, I assume as much. Cynical white people understand. Anti-imperialists take it in. Others—the good conscience—have their guts wrenched. The ensuing sentiment: hatred. I am exalted. Typically, I would seize this moment in the narrative to reassure the reader: "I am not homophobic and don't have any particular sympathy for Ahmadinejad." I will do no such thing. This is not the problem. The only real question is that of the Native Americans. My original wound. "Cowboys are the good guys and Indians are the bad guys." Sitting Bull was destroyed by this lie. The hero of the famous battle of Little Big Horn was assassinated in 1890. And his descendant, Leonard Peltier, languishes in a cell. His ancestors were shattered by this lie. It devastated them. To destroy it, each Native American would have had to knock on the door of each of the world's citizens to convince them, one by one, that the real aggressors were the cowboys and beg to be believed. And while they knocked painfully on each door:

The voice: "Where there's smoke there's fire. It's more complicated."

A large lump gathers deep in the Native American's throat and tears well up in his eyes. But because his faith is immense, some of us hear him knocking on the door.

"There are no homosexuals in Iran." This sentence, uttered in Bamako or Beijing, would, at best, be completely uninteresting, and at worst, merely unfortunate. But it is uttered at the heart of empire. In the kingdom of the *Innocents*. It is an arrogant indigenous man who speaks it. At a transitional moment in the history of the West: its decline. The aesthetics of the scene are all of this at once. First, its profound duality. "The Manicheanism of the colonist produces the Manicheanism of the colonized," said Fanon.[5] And then, it takes place in a famous leftist university, most likely at the pinnacle of progressive thought. In front of neoconservatives, it would have been a bit bland. What is Ahmadinejad saying? He isn't saying anything. He is lying, that's all. He is lying in all honesty. And this is huge. By lying and by taking responsibility for his lie in front of a crowd that knows he is lying, he is invincible. To the statement "There is no torture in Abu Ghraib," the echo answers: "There are no homosexuals in Iran." Persian rhetoric, usually used to enable white progressives, hits home. Both lies cancel each other out; the truth erupts. And good conscience disintegrates. It begins to cringe. Nothing but ugliness remains... and poets. The Left is ugly. So ugly. "Henceforth, the colonized know they have an advantage over them. They know that their temporary 'masters' are lying," wrote Césaire.[6] The Native American smiles and I smile too. We hold back our tears. To take pleasure in so little. An artisanal lie in the face of an imperial lie. Yes, it's pathetic.

Nouvel Obs: "What would you say to the French racist who is afraid?"
James Baldwin: "I would say hello."[7]

I ask myself. You are afraid? Why? You are afraid of us. You are afraid.... It's irrational. You belong to super-powerful nations that protect you. You are one of the peoples that dominate the planet. There is a plethora of means that guarantee this power, starting with your abundant nuclear arsenals, and with their corollary, nuclear dissuasion, and the corollary's corollary, the treaty of non-proliferation. So, what are you afraid of?

You know what.

Some knowledge lies deep down at the bottom of your soul. In your greatest depths. This knowledge is passed on. A heritage. Otherwise, would you call it "a burden"? You know what crimes have been committed in your name, or with your complicity. It's not a memory that is immediately conscious. It is diffuse. It lies dormant. Sometimes, it opens an eye and quickly closes it again. Your eyes are wide shut. Fear is undefinable. It's the malaise of whiteness. The mind suppresses but the heart races. It recognizes in any non-white face, be it in the factory, at school, or in the street, a survivor of the colonial enterprise, at the same time as it recognizes the *possibility* of vengeance. This is why you are afraid. Must you be reassured? It would be futile, since your military arsenals haven't done the job.

You are afraid but you hold on to your comfort. This is your dilemma. You don't want to give up on the infinite privileges of colonial domination. Your privileges are material, statutory, institutional, political, symbolic. Within the same social standing, it is always better to be white. The first of your privileges, and by far the most precious, is life. It is priceless. It is protected by your morals, your laws, your weapons. Your death is a fatality that hurts your narcissism. On an individual level, you do not exist. You are a collective power. You exist only when upheld by national or imperial powers, which guarantee your supremacy. You are the absolute, the center, the universal. When you contemplate the world, you deplore the distance that the relative, the peripheral, and the particular must still travel to catch up with you. You know you're white when you marry a West Indian, when you share a *mafé* with your Senegalese friend, or when you walk around in Saint-Denis, Bamako, or Tangiers. You always know who's white. You always know who's not white. We too have the same knowledge. Paradoxically, you "discover" that you are white—especially the French—when we call you "white." In reality, you discover nothing.

You simply recoil at being named, situated, your guilt thereby uncovered and your immunity rendered vulnerable.

Whiteness is an unassailable fortress. Your architects designed it to confront all kinds of obstacles and resolve all kinds of contradictions. Every white person builds this fortress. Sometimes, one must kill and starve. Sometimes one must caress. In principle, one must take and steal. First, like a gangster, a brute, or a thug. With time, one learns good manners. Between the final beneficiary and the first person to be dispossessed is a whole chain of intermediaries. From link to link, from strata to strata, manners are perfected. The dispossessed indigenous person is vulgar. The white dispossessor is refined. At one end of the chain is barbarism, at the other, civilization. It's good to be innocent. It allows you to play at being candid. And to always be on the right side. Because in addition to being innocent, you are humanists. This is not the least of your talents. You have played this part with unequaled verve and mastery. I can do nothing else but bow to you.

Humanism is one of the centerpieces of your immune system. "An organism's immune system is a biological system consisting of an organized set of recognition and defense mechanisms, which distinguish between the 'self' from the 'non-self'[...]. What is identified as a 'non-self' molecule is destroyed."[8] Or: "The organism's complex defense system against illnesses; one of the immune system's properties is its capacity to recognize foreign bodies and activate defense measures."[9]

Attacked on all sides, provoking hatred all over the world, cornered into justifying your conquests, weakened by the multi-faceted resistance movements and especially by the struggles for independence, confronted to your intrinsic ugliness and to what you consider to be the paroxysm of your madness—Nazism—you have had to equip yourselves with an apparatus for global and structural defense that would ensure the continuation of the imperial project as well as the longevity and survival of your social body. This political-ideological apparatus is the *white immune system*. Through it, many antibodies have been secreted. Among them, humanism and the monopoly of ethics. You are the greatest antiracists. Haven't you, time and time again, celebrated the struggle of Martin Luther King against segregation? You are the most appalled by anti-Semitism. Haven't you sacrificed Céline, Barbie, and so many others a million times over on the pyres of the public square? You are the greatest anticolonialists. Didn't you prostrate yourselves before the courage and abnegation of Nelson Mandela? You are the most sensitive to Africa's "under-development." Didn't you pour tons of rice into that continent of misery, then advocate that the African people should be taught to fish rather than simply receive the gift of fish? You are the most involved in humanitarian causes. Didn't you sing for Africa? You are the greatest feminists. Didn't you devote your attention to the fate of Afghan women and promise to save them from the Taliban's claws? You are the most anti-homo-phobic. Didn't you rush head first to the defense of homosexuals in the Arab world? How could we possibly climb to your level? We are gnomes, you are giants.

You even sometimes claim to have *carried our suitcases*. You never miss an opportunity to remind us of this. Those who did it are our brothers and we owe them respect, but may I suggest that in fact, they never carried *our* suitcases. Never. They only carried their own... or yours, if you prefer. When asked to define the black problem, Richard Wright answered: "There is no black problem in the United States, there is only a white problem."[10] So I repeat the question: Why won't you finally carry your own suitcases? Because, if your history made you white, nothing is forcing you to stay that way.

> Bertrand Poirot-Delpech: "Does being white make one guilty? A sort of original sin?"
> Jean Genet: "I don't think of it as original sin; in any case not the one the Bible talks about. No, it's a sin that is completely deliberate."

BPD: "You didn't want to be born white, from what I can tell?"

JG: "Oh, in that sense, by being born white and being against whites, I have played all the boards at once. I'm thrilled when whites are hurting and I'm protected by the power of whites, since I too have white skin and blue eyes, or green, or gray."[11]

"It's a sin that is completely deliberate."

And old sins have long shadows.

I will readily concede this to you: you didn't choose to be white. You're not really guilty. Just responsible. If there is a burden that deserves to be borne, it's this one. The white race was invented to fulfill the needs of what would soon become your bourgeois class, because any alliance between slaves who were not yet black and proles who were not yet white was becoming a threat. Within the context of the American conquest, nothing predestined your ancestors to become white. On the contrary, all the conditions for the alliance between slaves and proletarians were present. It was a close one. In the face of this threat, those who would become the American bourgeoisie offered you a *deal*: to give you a stake in the trafficking of black people and make you ally yourselves with the exploitation of slaves. This is how the bourgeoisie invented common interests between itself and you, or your ancestors, if you prefer. This is how, progressively, by institutionalizing itself, the white race was invented. In fact, race, in the hands of the white bourgeois, is an instrument of management; in your hands, it is a salary, a distinction. Since then, what has separated us is neither more nor less than a conflict of interest between races, a conflict which is as powerful and structured as class conflict.

You've surely understood that I am not addressing you all equally. Numerous contradictions flow through you, including class. I am speaking only to these two categories among you: first, the proles, the unemployed, the peasants, the lumpen, who are progressively giving up on politics or inexorably slipping away from communism toward the extreme Right—regional minorities that have been crushed by a few centuries of fanatical centralism, and all of those who have fallen through the cracks, whether you like us or not. In a word, those that have been sacrificed by the Europe of the markets and by the state, both of which are becoming less and less about welfare and increasingly more cynical. And then, I'm addressing the revolutionaries, who are aware of the coming barbarism. Because it is only a few steps away from us. It is going to devour us. I feel like the time has come. Everything has an end. Your immune system is weakening. The lacquer is fading. Your social status is weakening. Capitalism, in its neoliberal form, continues to carry out its relentless task. It chips away at your social benefits, or, more accurately, at your privileges. Up until now, to save social democracy, in other words, to save your white middle class interests, you have exploited us. You ordered us to vote tactically. We obeyed. To vote socialist. We obeyed. Then to defend republican values. We obeyed. And above all not to play into the game of the National Front. We obeyed. In other words, we sacrificed ourselves to save you. Two terrible world wars left you with painful memories. "Never again!" You continue to squall this wishful thinking like a broken record, but these psalms have no more impact than the chirping of birds. You no longer want to feed the belly of the beast because, in the past, it devoured you, except it is this beast that feeds you and with which you will devour the world. So, you support the status quo. We pay the bill. While your weak stomach holds on to social democracy, your radicals start to stir. A part of you turns toward fascism, the other toward us. But this alliance between equals disgusts you. Usually, you tolerate us only if you have also sponsored us. But it's possible that when the bell tolls, you won't have a choice but to take us into consideration. Of course, you'll always have the choice of fascism, but like all choices, it isn't inevitable. I will take advantage of this moment of intimacy to tell you a secret.

I despise the Left, which surely despises you just as much, if not more. I despise it fiercely. To the vulgar among you: to your resentment, your fear of downgrading, your frustrations—legitimate or not—the Left has opposed the yellow hand of SOS Racism, a kind of talisman or maybe even a garlic clove? What a joke! Pretending to fight you, it fed you. Sometimes, it outstripped you. You remained fascinated in the face of the Left's Islamophobic passion. As for the working class Left, it has given up on you. You have given up on it. For this, I don't blame you. Nor for the rest of it, either, because I am not a moralist. You find refuge from this Europe that betrays you and that some don't hesitate to qualify as a "counter-revolution by anticipation" in the arms of the holy nation.[12] But how long do you think that the nation will protect you against the assaults of capital? Not much longer.

If things were as they should be, the most conscientious of you would be tasked with making us a proposition to avoid the worst. But things are not as they should be. It is incumbent on us to fulfill this task. Instead of a white, embittered, and egotistical nation, have you considered a domestic internationalism, which would be better armed against the ravages of neoliberalism?[13] I cannot, for the life of me, conceive of what offer would be "generous" enough to make you consider this perspective. What would be convincing enough to make you give up on defending the racial interests that comfort you out of your downgrading and thanks to which you have the satisfaction of dominating (us)? Other than peace, I don't know what it would be. By peace, I mean the opposite of "war," of "blood," of "hatred." I mean: living together peacefully. And then, I remember that surrealistic scene in the film *Brazil*. In it, a white, bourgeois family feasts in a hip restaurant. All around them, a few meters away, are horrific scenes of war, of mutilated, dismembered bodies. You are the family; the war, of course, is the millions of dead in Iraq, in Congo, and in Rwanda, but even closer to us geographically, it's September 11th, or the attacks against *Charlie Hebdo*, the Kosher supermarket or the Bataclan, unemployment, the martyrdom of Greece. The barbarism to come won't spare us, but it won't spare you either.

You always pass right by us and often miss us. I no longer believe that this series of missed encounters between you and immigration were simply due to coincidence. I am beginning to understand that the site of a real encounter can only happen at the crossroads of our mutual interests—the fear of civil war and chaos—the site where races could annihilate each other and where it is possible to imagine our equal dignity. Because I tend to give in to sentimentality, I wonder if this isn't the space of love. Revolutionary love. Romantic souls will say that love is always disinterested. Precisely. How can we envision love between us if the privilege of the one relies on the oppression of the other?

From this point on, everything would be permissible. Why should we remain cloistered within the borders of the nation state? Why not rewrite history, denationalize it, deracialize it? Your patriotism forces you to identify yourself with your state. You celebrate its victories and lament its defeats. But how are we to make history together when our victories are your defeats? If we invite you to share in Algerian Independence and the victory in Dien Bien Phu with us, would you agree to break your solidarity with your warmongering states? We have a more interesting proposition. It was made to you in the past, a long time ago, by the late C.L.R. James, who was already a believer in revolutionary love:

> These are my ancestors, these are my people. They are yours too if you want them.[14]

James offers you the memory of his negro ancestors who rose against you and who, by freeing him, freed you. In essence, James says, change the

Pantheon, this is how we will make History and build the Future together. It sounds a whole lot better than "our ancestors the Gauls," don't you think?

One day, during a visit to France, my grandmother went to the hospital to see my father—her son—who was recovering from a surgery and shared his room with a man—a white man who was probably close to dying. Full of pity, she bent over him and kissed him, like a mother would kiss her own son. Later, she regretted it. Had she sinned by kissing a nonbeliever? Would God punish her and close the gates of Heaven to her? Had she betrayed him? I remember that my father had doubted, he had reassured her, but had left it up to God Almighty.

That memory has remained instructive for me. First, in the spontaneous impulse, the kiss, there is a promise of forgetting and overcoming the colonial dispute between my grandmother—who lived through the long colonial night and the torments of the Algerian War—and this one-time son. The moment is fleeting but real. Then, there is the return of indigenous rationality, of resistance. He isn't really one of us.

> The Negro came to the white man for a roof or for five dollars or for a letter to the judge; the white man came to the Negro for love. But he

was not often able to give what he came seeking. The price was too high; he had too much to lose. And the Negro knew this, too. When one knows this about a man, it is impossible for one to hate him, but unless he becomes a man—becomes equal—it is also impossible for one to love him.[15]

War and peace have a price. It must be paid.

3

YOU, THE JEWS

"*Who is Hitler?*"
My cousin from the bled[1]

One day, an Israeli judge, Moshe Landau, famous for having presided over Adolf Eichmann's trial, said: "I hate Arabs, they remind me so much of Sephardic [Jews]." Exquisite perfidy, isn't it? It makes me want to paraphrase him: I hate Jews, they remind me so much of Arabs.

It's true, you are very familiar to me. Not so much because we are both "People of the Book," or because we supposedly have a common ancestor, the prophet Abraham. This genealogy doesn't speak to me in a political way. What makes us real "cousins" is your relationship to white people. Your condition within the West's geopolitical borders. When I look at you, I see us. Your existential contours are drawn. Like us, you are entrenched. You can recognize a Jew not because he calls himself one, but because of his willingness to meld into whiteness, to support his oppressor, and to want to embody the canons of modernity. Like us.

> If the Jew is fascinated by Christians it is not because of their virtues, which he values little, but because they represent anonymity, humanity without race.[2]

I could recognize you anywhere. Your zeal betrays you. Some of you even combat anti-white racism. And with such energy. For god's sake. The more you do, the more you distinguish yourselves, and the more suspect you are. In comparison, consider the soft tranquility of those who have nothing to prove. The Innocents. You are not the *real* chosen people. You are being lied to. But you know this. None of your ideological choices completely protect you; you are safe nowhere. Like us, you spend your lives oscillating between self-disillusionment and self-affirmation. In the end, you know that France's so-called Philo-Semitism is a mask. You are Jewish, so you doubt.

> I don't exactly know what it means to be Jewish, what being Jewish means to me. This may be stating an obvious fact, but it's a

mediocre fact, a mark, but a mark that doesn't tie me to anything in particular, to anything concrete: it is not a sign of belonging, it is not tied to a belief, a religion, a practice, a culture, a folklore, a history, a destiny, a language. Rather, it would be an absence, a question, a questioning, a hesitation, a worry: a worried certainty behind which the contours of another certainty are drawn, one that is abstract, heavy, unbearable: that of having been designated as Jewish...[3]

So, you doubt. Can I even reproach you for this? I have to admit that your ideological choices, as disparate as they may be, are determined by your condition. It is this doubt that makes you internationalists. It is this doubt that makes you Zionists. It is this same doubt that makes you apologists of the republican myth.

In fact, it's true, you were really chosen by the West. For three cardinal missions: to solve the white world's moral legitimacy crisis, which resulted from the Nazi genocide, to outsource republican racism, and finally to be the weaponized wing of Western imperialism in the Arab world. Can I allow myself to think that in your heart, it is the part that loves the white world that pushed you to sign this deal with the devil? This is how, in the span of fifty years, you went from being pariahs, to being, on the one hand, *dhimmis of the Republic* to satisfy the internal needs of the nation state, and on the other, *Senegalese riflemen* to satisfy the needs of Western imperialism.

Dhimmis of the Republic. Does it shock you? I understand. On Islamic land, the dhimmi was the Christian or Jewish subject of a Muslim leader who, in exchange for a toll, received the leader's protection and hospitality. That's right; the dhimmi's status was inferior to that of the dominant group. He governed premodern societies. It would be anachronistic to judge him—as you are already tempted to do— through a contemporary lens. It's useless to try to escape by that route. I am merely providing this little historical reminder so that we can observe together the strange similarities between this statutory inferiority and your condition, here, on Catholic-secular land. You heap insults on the dhimmi under Islamic law, while praising him under the republican regime. Ah! How horrible were those sultans, emirs, and khalifs back in the day! Yet how good and strong are your protectors today. You have given up on depriving white people of their throne and instead pledged allegiance to them. You have abandoned the "universalist" struggle by accepting the Republic's racial pact: white people on top, as the legitimate body of the nation, us as pariahs at the bottom, and you, as buffer. But in an uncertain, uncomfortable, in-between. Of course, dhimmis are better than *Untermenschen*, but you remain at the mercy of the political climate. Luckily, you are rewarded. From now on, you are stakeholders in the "Judeo-Christian civilization." Admit it. It's sad that this rehabilitation has been conditioned by genocide, by your partial self-expulsion from Europe and the Arab world for Israel, and by your renunciation to fully reclaim a France which is, nevertheless, yours.

I don't know if you realize to what extent you are precious? Being dhimmis isn't so bad, but being infantrymen of Zionist imperialism is even better. They are strong, aren't they? I will happily admit that I admire our oppressors. It is the privilege of the dominant class to know our weaknesses. To be part of the masters' race. That's what we all want. So, then, they gave you Israel. Two birds one stone: they got rid of you as pretenders to the nation and as historical revolutionaries, and made you into the most passionate defenders of the empire on Arab soil. What they did was even more vicious. They managed to make you trade your religion, your history, and your memories for a colonial ideology. You abandoned your Jewish, multi-secular identities; you despise Yiddish and Arabic and have entirely given yourselves over to the Zionist identity. In only fifty years. It is as if sorcerers had put a spell on you. Is Zionism not another name for your capitulation?

And yet, you resisted for a long time.
The Wandering Jew is a clock. Listen to his limp, his slow, tired step; it never stops.[4]

But you let yourself be won over, slowly, such that a tenacious bias was born: all Jews are Zionists. Now, if you aren't a Zionist, you have to prove it. You, who dreamt of melding into the "universal," have now become Jewish again in the Sartrian sense of the word. But for me, this isn't the worst part. After all, your renunciations are your business, and yours alone. The worst part is my gaze, when in the street, I pass by a child wearing a kippah. That fleeting moment when I stop to look at him. The worst part is the disappearance of my indifference toward you, the possible prelude to my internal ruin.

The voice: "The belly is still fertile from which the foul beast sprang."[5]

"But who is Hitler?" That's Boujemaa, my Algerian cousin, speaking. I almost fell off my seat. My cousin doesn't know who Hitler is. An idiot. I blame his ignorance on the Algerian educational system, which is obviously rotten, as are supposedly rotten the people from the *bled*. Hitler is someone I know intimately. I met him on the benches of the schools of the Republic. I also met Anne Frank there, whom I cried over greatly. Just as much as I abhorred the man of the final solution. The man of the Judeocide. School trained me well. When I heard an expression like: "Stop eating like a Jew!" I would cast a dirty look. I was the idiot. Thanks to Boujemaa, I learned something. For the South, the Shoah—if I dare say so—is nothing but a "detail." It's not even visible in the rear-view mirror. Truth be told, this history is not really mine and I will hold it at a distance so long as the history and the life of the wretched of the earth will also remain nothing but "a detail." That's why I say this as I look you straight in the eyes: I will not go to Auschwitz.

You must think that I am insulting you and that I am uneducated. That's false. My cousin's words are precious to me. And I think that they can be equally precious for you if you make the effort to listen. What is he saying? Things that cleanse. We need to repatriate anti-Semitism, identify its geopolitical territory, its original locus. Anti-Semitism is European. It is a product of modernity. The Dreyfus affair, the impetuous development of anti-Jewish movements in the interwar period, the rise of Nazism, and the Vichy regime, all demonstrate anti-Semitism's deep-seated roots in Europe. It has confined you to the lower echelons of the hierarchy of honors, but it is not universal. It is circumscribed in space and time. No, the Inuit, the Dogon, and the Tibetans are not anti-Semitic. They aren't Philo-Semitic either. They don't care about you. I wouldn't say the same about the Arab-Muslim world, since we've been involved for several centuries. But we aren't anti-Semitic either. There may be many conflicts between us, but they aren't Nazi in nature. They could be religious or theological. They might have to do with the political structuring of our original societies and of relative distributions of powers. More often than not they are colonial. But that's it. And that is already a heavy burden to have to relieve ourselves of. You who are Sephardic, you can't act as though the Crémieux Decree hadn't existed. You can't ignore the fact that France made you French to tear you away from us, from your land, from your Arab-Berber identity. If I dare say so, from your Islamic identity. Just as we have been dispossessed of you. If I dare say so, of our Jewish identity. Incidentally, I can't think about North Africa without missing you. You left a void that we will never be able to fill, and for that I am inconsolable. Your alterity becomes more pronounced and your memory fades.

I really like my cousin. He's like a clearing in the middle of the forest. When I think about all the crooks who burglarize our history, who break into it, for instance, to honor us on the grounds that we protected you against Vichy. We are raised to the rank of the JUST. A supreme honor! And yet, what an insult. What perversity. Like spitting in our face. Must we be spineless to accept such an honor? For, if the Just who have risked their lives to protect the Jews exist on European land, it is in large part because their fellow citizens were anti-Semites. But what does this distinction mean for us, who did not collaborate and who also lived under the yoke of the West? Because to make an indigenous person Just is to invent a contrast, to create an opposition from scratch between him and his blood brothers; it is to brand the indigenous mass with the seal of anti-Semitic infamy. If Mohamed V was Just, the Moroccans were not. Bastards! Stop sullying us. Manipulation has only one goal: to share the Shoah, to dilute it, to deracinate Hitler and move him to the colonized populations, and in the end, to exonerate white people. To universalize anti-Semitism, to make of it an a-temporal and stateless phenomenon, is to kill two birds with one stone: it is to justify the hold-up of Palestine as well as the repression of indigenous people in Europe. And in all decency, the only people who could really receive the medal of the Just are your white suitcase carriers. But were they expecting a reward? It's in such poor taste to think so. Why offend their modesty with this kind of vulgar staging? I'm slow off the mark, but all this makes me think of Charlie Chaplin. Did you know that his whole life, he never denied a Jewishness of which he was strongly suspected, even though he wasn't Jewish? For him, to refute this rumor would have been to play the anti-Semite's game. Do you see what I'm saying?

I digress. I don't yet feel like you are completely convinced by my cousin Boujemaa. And yet, the word of the oppressed is gold. Whether you want it or not, it will always rise before you to prevent you from sleeping in peace, because ever since modernity has taken a bite out of you, you have become, *nolens volens*, part of our oppressors. You are the "new Jews."

I'll give Césaire a try. Who knows, perhaps he will find the words to convince you. With his poet language, he invites us to attempt a decolonial reading of the Nazi genocide—the Shoah.

> [T]hat they tolerated that Nazism before it was inflicted on them, that they absolved it, shut their eyes to it, legitimized it, because, until then, it had been applied only to non-European peoples; that they have cultivated that Nazism, that they are responsible for it, and that before engulfing the whole of Western, Christian civilization in its reddened waters, it oozes, seeps, and trickles from every crack.[7]

> And yet, through the mouths of the Sarrauts and the Bardes, the Mullers and the Renans, through the mouths of all those who considered—and consider—it lawful to apply to non-European peoples "a kind of expropriation for public purposes" for the benefit of

nations that were stronger and better
equipped, it was already Hitler speaking![7]

Before mass crimes were tested in Europe, they were
first tested in the Americas, in Africa, in Asia. To
dehumanize a race, to destroy it, to make it disappear
from the surface of the earth, is already inscribed in
the colonial genes of National Socialism. Hitler was
nothing if not a good student. If the techniques of
mass massacre revealed all their efficiency in the con-
centration camps, it is because they had been tested
on us, and thus made all the more efficient; and if
white ferociousness came down on you with such
savagery, it is because European populations closed
their eyes to the "tropical genocides."

The voice: There is a uniqueness to the Shoah.

The risk of removing its singularity from the Nazi
genocide is real, and you would be right to point it
out. The negationist tendency looms large with the
anti-Semites. But to have let the commemoration
of the Nazi genocide become a "European civil
religion" makes one fear for the worst, because one
either has or does not have faith in religion.[8] In
this context, atheism produces imitators, it repro-
duces itself. With all due respect to Claude
Lanzmann, the time of blasphemy has come.
Against his "Here, there is no why"[9] we must

instead continue to question ourselves about the genealogy of this crime. If you really fear negationism, it is urgent to lay to rest these ideologies that glorify you as supreme victims and create hierarchies of horror. You must do justice to the Roma, the homosexuals, the Soviets, and the communists who died alongside your own people, and you must just as urgently recognize one of Nazism's origins: the trans-Atlantic slave trade and colonialism. We could then adopt this thought of Rosa Luxemburg's: "I feel at home in the entire world, wherever there are clouds and birds and tears."[10] Or, in other words, we will all together and more loudly proclaim that no, the Shoah, like all mass crimes, will never be a "detail."

Abdelkebir Khatibi is not as famous as Césaire though he deserves to be. His vision acts as a deregulator of Zionist mechanisms. "Essence precedes existence," he writes. "Arab essence precedes the existence of Israel," he adds. And he pulverizes Sartre's bad conscience, which he defines as: "The unhappy conscience secretes a very efficient machine of ignorance, ignorance of self and other, for the initial duality inherent to the unhappy conscience is reversed: by expropriating Palestinians, the Zionist relieves his conscience by offering it his sin and his misfortune." He continues: "In a rush to give his point of view on the Israeli-Arab conflict, Sartre repeatedly answers that his position is dual (it is at once pro-Israel and pro-Palestinian) and that he experiences this question in the greatest state of devastation and embarrassment. A dual position that we might define as a fake neutrality and an alibi, which serve as an indictment of the Sartrian system. This system, as we all know, is founded on a responsible morality, which is able to surpass and harm itself. This indictment occurs at discrete points, it does not question the entirety of the system [...]. What I am trying to demonstrate here is that Sartre, by becoming a conformist, ultimately has the attitude of a conditional Zionist, and that he finds himself cornered into not granting his devastation a positively revolutionary meaning. He experiences, in his own way, the terror of an unhappy consciousness."[11]

And as if Khatibi wasn't enough, there are also the words of the Palestinians. Listen to them: You are like a parachutist who, having landed in the middle of the night in an unknown place, wakes up in the morning and asks himself: "What are all these Arabs doing around me?" You, who are stateless? You, who lived in Poland, were you not Polish? You who lived in Yemen, were you not Yemenites? You, who lived on this Palestinian land, were you not Palestinians? You, Hebrews? Are you certain of it? Are we Muslims, Christians, and Jews of Palestine, not the real descendants of the Hebrews, who you claim to be your ancestors? Are you like those Frenchmen who mythologize their so-called Gaulic descent? Us, anti-Semites? You criticize us for cursing you as Jews, but is it not in this capacity that you colonized us? You reproach us for giving into the essentialism of the Jews, but your German oppressors, did you insult them in prose or in rhyme? Look at yourself in the mirror and you will see us. We will keep standing until the very last of us drops because the greatest offence that was done to us is the denial of history. We will resist in its name.

"Who will live in our house after us, father?"
"It will stay just as we left it, my child."
He touched his keys as if he were touching his limbs and calmed down.[12]

The words of the colonized are dense. They are powerful. They do not lie. But deep down inside of me, I know that they won't satisfy you. They shake you up, they gnaw you, they upset your conscience, but what will make you sway definitively is self-love. First of all, the respect you owe your martyrs and the memory of their painful and haggard eyes. The memory of their scrawny bodies in front of the gates of the camps, which they latched onto with despair. But also, the intolerable instrumentalization of their plight toward ideological ends, which today makes up the backbone of Israeli nationalism. I rule entirely in your favor. It's true, it is to your dead that you will have to answer to.

Second of all, your insecurity within the white world. Philo-Semitism gets old. Just like paternalism. Too slimy to be true. They are two forms of republican racism, which are in fact nothing but compromises between the extreme Right's radical racism and the preservation of the white nation state.

As I've already told you, you are both familiar and strange to me. Familiar because of your insoluble non-whiteness within anti-Semitic whiteness, but strange because you are whitened, integrated into a superior echelon of the racial hierarchy. To be honest, between us, everything is still possible. I might be optimistic, but that's my own choice. We have a common destiny in the same way that we potentially have a common political future. This will depend on what part of your personality, fashioned by "modernity," will win out: Zionism and the comfort of dhimmitude or the consciousness of your eternal deferment. Should you prefer the second option, we could walk some of the way together. All the conditions are in place. We are living in a transitional moment in our history. On the international chessboard, Israel disappoints the empire, Iran is imposing itself as a regional power, and the Zionist transplant never took hold in the Arab world, and never will, god willing. In Europe, nationalisms prosper in the shadow of the crisis of civilization, and take as their targets the Muslim "Semites." How much longer do you expect to escape the worst by relying on the ability of the sycophants of the flag to distinguish between a Muslim "Semite" and a "Semitic Jew?"

Let's put all our cards on the table. At this point, I could be satisfied with tormenting you and charting my course, because today you and I are not located on the same level on the ladder of oppressions. As a result, there is a conflict of interest between us. That much is true. *But we have this in common that we do not make up the legitimate bodies of the nation.* There is a common struggle that could be the deconstruction of the racial and republican pact that is at the foundation of the French nation. It benefits white Europeans and Christians and privileges European Jews within the Jewish world, at the expense of Eastern Jews. More and more of you are aware of this. The problem is that often your doubts comfort you in the idea that a national Jewish center is of vital necessity. I'll tell you this too, I am not a moralist. You are free to make this choice. But because of this freedom you will be held accountable. You are condemned to the binary: West or Third World, whiteness or decolonization, Zionism or anti-Zionism. You have the choice to prolong your servitude within ethnically divided or racist nationalisms, or, on the contrary, to free yourselves from the hold of the French nation state and the Israeli nation state. In other words, to follow in the footsteps of the proud militants of the Bund[13] and to continue their dream of liberation.

Whether you like it or not, anti-Zionism will be, along with the indictment of the nation state, the primary site of this endgame. It will be the site of the historical confrontation between us, the opportunity for you to identify your real enemy. *Because fundamentally, it's not with us that you must be reconciled but with white people.*[14] We stand before a fool's game, in which we are the celebrities playing the main roles. Jews and Arabs, those terrible and turbulent children who exhaust themselves reconciling the good Christian souls. While the main actor is white: the West. Someone will retort that Herzl was a Jew. Sure, except that *the question is not who had the idea of Zionism first but who realized it.* Anti-Zionism will also be the site of the historical confrontation between you and white people, the opportunity for the latter to ask you three times for forgiveness: first, for the genocide, second, for not restoring, after 1945, your full and unconditional European citizenship, and finally, for gifting you an open-air prison: Israel. Anti-Zionism, finally, will be the site of the historical confrontation between us and white people, the opportunity for the latter to ask our forgiveness for the cynicism with which they have absolved themselves of their crimes carried out at our expense. Anti-Zionism is that territory in which the two primary victims of the Israeli project come to light: the Palestinians and the Jews. It is also where its primary beneficiary appears: the West. When white people break with blissful Philo-Semitism, they take the shortest route to end anti-Semitism. Not only the extreme Right's anti-Semitism, the vulgar fascists' anti-Semitism. The Republic's anti-Semitism. The anti-Semitism at the heart of the democrats, the one that they have never managed to uproot and whose awakening they constantly fear, because they have never given up on whiteness. This is what condemns them to track anti-Semitism everywhere, even where it isn't, and to wander along the precipice, at the bottom of which the "foul beast" awaits them, patient and eager. When you break with Zionism, you take the shortest route to put an end to the infernal cycle in which Zionism and anti-Semitism feed off each other endlessly, and in which you will always lose yourself. As for us, anti-Zionism is our country of asylum. Under its high patronage, we resist integration through anti-Semitism all the while pursuing the struggle for the liberation of the wretched of the earth.

On this matter—you are going to hate me—you owe us "toothless anti-Semites" a debt. When some of us, unpolished, invite themselves into a republican debate with their hiking boots on, they are useful to you, in a certain way. When, for instance, they challenge the memory of the genocide, they are touching on something that is far more sensitive than the memory of the Jews. They are challenging the temple of the sacred: white good conscience. The site where the West confiscates human ethics and turns it into its universal and exclusive monopoly. The home of white dignity. The bunker of abstract humanism. The benchmark according to which is measured subalterns' level of civilization. In fact, indigenous people, impolite and rebellious against this rule, from the moment they contest it, reveal family secrets. If we are jealous of you, it is because we covet your place in the heart of white people. Our desire for legitimization will doom us, but by contesting your status as favorite, we lay bare the illegitimacy of white rule and, with the same movement, the existence of the white prince, the real authority.

I have said this before. I refuse the honors and prefer the discretion of anemones to the fanfare of bugles. And yet, it is a historical fact. Many Muslims, be they individuals or authorities, have saved Jews without ever boasting about it. I would like to invite you to meditate on these words by Dieudonné that trouble my conscience. In one of his shows he repeats the remarks of another French humorist who apparently said: "It is unworthy of France that a man like Dieudonné can still express himself." Dieudonné replied:

As a Jew, he said that this reminded him of some of the darker times in history, this reminded him of the Thirties. Fuck! He said he was waiting for an official apology from me. So, I am taking advantage of this opportunity to tell him that he can shove my apology up his ass, and that I just want to let him know that if the wind blows a certain way and we end up in a climate like the Thirties, he better not come hide in my cave. In the case of a rematch, I'll give him up to the authorities immediately.[15]

I think he needs to be taken seriously. These are not the words of a mere jester, but the product of his time. This rotten system is turning you into monsters, just like it is turning us into villains. And yet, its task is not complete. I know the people of my race well. Though we may be battered and terribly damaged, we still have a big heart and a certain practice of human nobility; but for how much longer? I will take my leave of you now, but not without entrusting you with two of my certitudes first, and humbly, making you a "generous offer":

You are losing your historical friends.
You are still in the ghetto.
Why don't we got out of there together?

4

WE, INDIGENOUS WOMEN

"How brave!"
A white woman admiring a *beurette* escaped
from the familial gulag.[1]

"You will never shave off your father's mustache!"
That's my mother speaking.

All my life has been spent obeying this order,
fearing it, sanctifying it, avoiding it, defying it,
mocking it, evading it…and then obeying it once
again. And so on and so forth. My father passed.
With his beautiful mustache. I am relieved. I even
feel a certain degree of naïve pride.

My body does not belong to me.

No moral magisterium will make me endorse a
law conceived by and for white feminists.

Recite! "Ana hit ou oueld ennass khitt."[2] On my
left thigh, three marks made with a razor blade and

covered in kohl to dry up the blood. It's a patriarchal rite that overtakes your body, chains it to a
lineage of ancestors. My paternal grandmother
approves. I belong to her. My maternal grandmother approves. I belong to her. My grandfathers,
fallen martyrs, approve. I belong to them. My
father approves, I belong to him. As for my mother,
let's not even go there; she's the one who put the
cuffs around my wrists. I belong to her. The blood
has dried. The scar will be indelible. I belong to my
family, my clan, my neighborhood, my race; I
belong to Algeria, to Islam. I belong to my history
and God willing, I will belong to my descendants.
"When you are married, in cha Allah, you will say:
Ana khitt ou oueld ennass hitt.[3] Then, you will
belong to your husband."

The voice: It's awful.

France is very strong. It has declared war on my
parents. The battle is arduous. France wants to
tear my body away from them, colonize it. France
is voracious. It wants me all to itself. "They are
barbarians!" France yells and yells. I hear this
everywhere. "They are barbarians!" But the scar
doesn't wear off. My ancestors won the game.

   I have nothing to hide of what takes place at
home. From the best to the most rotten. In this
scar are all my impasses as a woman. The world is

cruel toward us. The family honor rests on my dead father's mustache, my father whom I love and whom France destroyed. I am going to have to take care of it and look after him. We alone know the price of the beaten down colonized's mustache. My brother is ashamed of his father. My father is ashamed of his son. Neither of them is still standing. I pick up their fallen virility, their scorned dignity, their exile. Through them, I pick up my mother. No, my body does not belong to me. My mother continues to exercise sovereignty over it. But I am a conscious accomplice. I share the reins to my life with her, with my entire tribe. In any case, even if I had removed them, it would have been to hand them over to white people. I'd rather die. I would rather deal with it... And play it by ear. Racism is perverse. It is a devil. See how, in its presence, everything becomes paradoxical and hazy. Quick, a flash light! The white morgue. Swollen with itself, it underestimated our men. Is racism that dumb? It holds its opponent in such contempt that it imagines him to be harmless. It imagines that our men are but inert and disabled bodies. You arrive, you steal their wives and they reward you with a "thank you bwana."[4] Damn! In reality, they exist, they breathe, they form a group, a social body with interests to defend. An active body that defends its privileges. So, let's take it from the top. When, for example, the white patriarch exclaims, "Oh, indigenous man, I am handsome, strong, intelligent, far more so than you will ever be, and I am going to take your wife away from you," he pictures a defeatist man, who will answer: "Please, go ahead, do as you wish." He doesn't know that he is speaking to an adversary, a fearsome enemy who will protect what belongs to him. And that is what the indigenous male will do. He will defend his male interests. His resistance will be relentless: "We are not fags!" This is how we will become a battle field. We will be battered and quartered. Submissive to some, treacherous to others.

And yet, "Georgette's" father had warned us:

> Let the sea swallow you all! You're not listening to me! You think what your teacher tells you is true, is that right! No good can come from them, none! And if you don't believe me, you'll see…. Remember what your father told you. When I'm gone, you'll see for yourself! You'll say: my father, he was right! But it's too late…. And you, you've come to sabotage my children's education. You're the poison in this house. This poison, I feed it, dress it, care for it when it's sick. I slog around all day for nothing. But me, I'm not Si Slimane! His wife and his children shat on his white beard. He worked his whole

life for them…. At work like a dog, like a rat…. In the end, she rose the children against him. I'd told 'em: if you marry a woman from here, it's gonna be a disaster. I married a woman from my village, and it's the biggest disaster. Madame la Biquette, she wants to act like a Westerner. She's even worse than the mini-skirt fashion! But me, I'm not Si Slimane! I'll kill you all! One by one. I'm not afraid of the justice of men. I don't give a damn about justice here, about the justice of dogs…. I'm calmly writing the words of God in my daughter's notebook and look at what happens: your mother, she let the atomic bomb loose on my ass. When I brought her here, she didn't even know how to say hello-goodbye, now she breathes down my neck. The boss does it every day; and when I come home, it's your mother! She's messing with your minds…. But I'd prefer to kill you all. Or else, I'll take everyone to Marseille. You'll eat a dry pancake and an onion. That way, you'll understand that I'm the father![5]

Sisters, do you remember the television film *Pierre et Djemila*? Him, handsome, in love, considerate. White. Her, beautiful, in love, terrorized by her family. Arab. That film was intended for us, the daughters of immigrants. It spoke to us. It told us how detestable our families were and how desirable

French society was. A film that turned us away from our kind, from our fathers, those exploited *zoufris*[6] who painstakingly kept us alive, and our mothers, wives of immigrants, who painstakingly raised us. The film explained to us, their daughters, that they treated us badly and that we had only one way out: to tear ourselves away from them. In the beginning, I'll be honest with you, I believed in this old tune which accompanied us everywhere, insinuating itself into every pore, incrusting itself into your skin. You too, perhaps? And then I doubted, and in the end, I didn't go for it. But I could have, like so many of us did. There's no doubt that the teenager that I was had already benefitted from the experience of our older sisters who (often) broke their teeth on the mirage of the white prince charming. A spell which cost them almost nothing: tearing their families apart, the stigmatization of their mother who was guilty of having "badly raised" them, the shame that reflected on everyone but also the guilt, and the bad reputation…. How many of our sisters committed suicide, caught in the cross fire of these two patriarchies? The white patriarchy, conquering and self-assured, and the other, the indigenous patriarchy, dominated and desperate. A spell that proposed to turn all of us into accomplices, auxiliaries to the racist system that would wield the deathblow to this much-hated family from North Africa. All this barely two or three decades after the African independence movements. That old recipe hasn't aged a day. In fact, didn't it reach its climax with the blazing success of Ni Putes Ni Soumises?[7] The French elite are unique. Consider their relationship to the sexism of those who are at the top, the sexism of those who are at the bottom, and the sexism of those who are beneath those who are at the bottom. The high-powered France that did not hesitate to publish a photo of Simone de Beauvoir, naked, in the headlines of a major magazine to celebrate the centennial of her birth. Can you image Sartre, naked, on the cover of a serious magazine? Undoubtedly, this must be read as the expression of an altogether French sensibility. Artistic. Aesthetic. Who better than the French elite to see and discern that which, behind feminism, defines "the woman"? A self-satisfied, know-it-all elite, walking five inches above ground and obstinately indifferent to reality. A reality that is mistreated and despised in favor of a self-satisfaction that has no limits. From our standpoint, the spectacle is edifying. What do we see? First off, the near-total indifference of this elite to white patriarchy, which structures French society and determines the lives of millions of women. And yet, all evidence demonstrates that the condition of French women is deteriorating (rape, domestic violence, wage disparity, exploitation of female bodies for commercial ends...). Next, these elites form tight ranks to irrevocably denounce violence done to women in the suburbs, when the perpetrator is black or Arab. The sexism of guys in these neighborhoods is a barbarism without cause or origin. See, all these white male chauvinists who become feminists when the guy from the suburb[8] appears? There is no word harsh enough to crucify him, no compassion strong enough to sympathize with him. All of the white world has time and time again united with quavering voices against the bad guy from the projects. *Last but not least*, they demonstrate a near-unanimous class solidarity to support DSK and co.[9] and come up with the most outrageous extenuating circumstances for them. An elite that becomes one with its male chauvinism: it euphemizes white rape, voluntarily confuses rape and licentiousness, and ignores any kind of compassion vis-à-vis victims when the perpetrator is white and high-ranking. On the other hand, against our brothers, it's a real corrida: the matadors are let loose.

Under pressure, certain of our men slip on a white mask. They don't wear it well. It disfigures them for life. Do they question themselves about their violence against us? Yeah, sure. They are ugly because they abdicate their power only to please white people. Because we are subjected to their violence. They abdicate in the face of power. When they court a white woman, they are chivalrous, considerate, romantic. Qualities that are unimaginable within the privacy of our housing projects. I've come to prefer big fat machos who own up to it. I'm telling you sisters, we must take drastic action. It's not good for us when our men reform themselves at the behest of white people. Because in fact, they do not reform themselves. They pretend to. They are actors, playing their roles with more or less talent. If you chase away what is natural, it comes running right back. And we're the ones to suffer the consequences. As I am swimming in my own contradictions, I'll admit, I prefer the original to the copy. Because it's less the reality of masculine domination that poses a problem than its dehumanization. What's worse is that none of this is new. These black people bearing white masks have illustrious predecessors. It's funny but feminist pioneers in the Islamic world were... men: Qasim Amine, Mohammed Abduh, Tahar Haddad, Taha Hussein, Mohammed Rachid Rida....[10] Most female Muslim commentators are pleased with this phenomenon and see in it an exceptional humanism, a God-given philanthropy. This naiveté leaves me speechless. Why would men voluntarily abdicate their privileges? Why on earth would they encourage a struggle that threatens their power over women? In Europe, the first feminists were, quite naturally, women. Why has the Islamic world given birth to such incongruity?

It's no big mystery to me. The elite in these societies were already crushed by the thought of their civilizational "backwardness." Women's liberation, when it is extolled by men, can in no way be explained by a pro-women tropism, but more conclusively by the complex of indigeneity, shamed by colonial power and seeking to hoist itself up to the level of the so-called norms of the colonized. These guys exhaust me. Speaking of virility, have you noticed, sisters, the emotion that overtakes a white democrat when a guy from the suburbs declares his homosexuality in front of a camera and mic? To hear a shyster make his coming out: what a joy for the white civilizer, an endpoint for the backward, indigenous people. Because for a *khoroto*,[11] to make of one's sexuality a social and political identity is to enter modernity through the front door. The white man is on the edge of ecstasy. All of these words jostling each other at the threshold of the indigenous person's still archaic consciousness—which, though it is still archaic, is destined to a Man's fate—besiege him: "to take responsibility for oneself," "to be accomplished," "to realize oneself," "to tear off one's chains," and "to shatter all taboos." The indigenous person is surrounded but hypnotized. Sometimes, because his people are suffocating, he gives in. Immediately, he is carried to the pinnacle. I'm sick and tired of these worthless heroes. But the white democrat goes into a trance.

When he meets that unlikely character, his body shakes all over, he has an irrepressible desire to kiss him, to hold him in his arms and commune with him. Thanks to this unexpected conversion, he has accomplished his civilizing mission. He has just won a miraculous victory against an enemy, who petrifies and taunts him: the great and insolent Islamic virility. The one that is maddening. The one that has male chauvinists drooling. "They veil their wives. They can have four of them. The bastards!" We must stop lying to ourselves. When white people rejoice at an indigenous man's coming out, it's both out of homophobia and out of racism. As we all know, "the faggot" is not quite a "man," thus, the Arab who loses his virile power is not quite a man. *And that's good. It's really good.* And it's so reassuring. It goes without saying that the message is understood loud and clear on the other side of the highway as well. The virile and homophobic competition that takes place in the opposite camp will come as no surprise, and it will take great pleasure in overplaying sexuality, which is fabricated by the colonial gaze in the devious war between antagonistic and irreducible forces. But aside from this, apparently, within philanthropic circles, they are worried about our lot, us chicks. No kidding!

My sisters, we are entitled to ask ourselves questions, are we not? Why have white women and especially feminists, who have refined knowledge of the patriarchy, let themselves be recruited in this sacred union against guys from the suburbs? Were they bewitched? I will not have the weakness to believe that. The truth is that, caught in a conflict of interest, they privileged racial solidarity. Like Le Pen, they prefer their family to their neighbor.... As indigenous people, we have known, since *Pierre et Djemila*, that there are very few people who want our well-being. We are nothing but foils, instruments of white vanity. This hypocrites' dance nevertheless has a virtue. It forces us to return to the real, to resituate ourselves. It compels us to remain lucid. We chase away the myths; we dissipate the fog. Let's look at our parents, let's look at our brothers, let's look at the women from our neighborhoods. And let's observe the white elite. And then, let's rediscover our mothers, our fathers, and our brothers. Them, enemies? There is no simple answer to this question. I would be lying if I answered with a candid and irrevocable no. But I make the conscious choice to say no because my liberation will not be attained without theirs. Like Assata Shakur, I say: "We can never be free while our men are oppressed."[12] No, my body does not belong to me. I know today that my place is among my own people. More than an instinct, it is a political approach. But before becoming conscious knowledge, this return was accomplished through a collective will for survival and resistance. My consciousness comes from this. Our collective self reacted by creating its own immune system. What becomes of Djemila—what becomes of us— when the time of romance has passed and Pierre dumps her for other horizons? What becomes of her financial autonomy? What becomes of the indigenous woman, isolated and vulnerable in a hostile society that discriminates against her, exoticizes her, and instrumentalizes her? Will she find a refuge among her own people after her "treason"? Sometimes, yes, and sometimes, it will be difficult. Whatever happens, she will have been disgraced. Why then take this risk? This is the question we must answer, especially those of us coming from the lower classes. In other words, most of us. A friend was telling me: "I have never been a feminist. I never even thought about it. For me, feminism is like chocolate." Isn't that right! Reproaching us for not being feminists is like reproaching a poor person for not eating caviar. For, what leeway do we have between the white patriarchy and "our own," indigenous and dominated patriarchy? How should we act when the latter's survival strategy consists in exposing his pecs, making a display of his virility? This is the equation that the collective self has had to resolve. An I that has easily achieved the difficult compromise between integrity, the safety of the group, and the liberation of the individual. A compromise between indigenous men and women, which some African sisters have called "nego-feminism." In this struggle, we have not been passive. We have played our part, making do as best we could. Some of us distanced themselves from white men, some drew closer to them, not without imposing their own conditions, others demanded a conversion to Islam, others wore the hijab. All this for a number of reasons, which range for the search for spirituality to political resistance, by way of a strong self-awareness and awareness of one's dignity. After all, we are not merely bodies available for white male consumption. And we refuse for our bodies to be exploited by the society of the spectacle. At the same time, we are rebuilding ties to ourselves. We belong to the "community" and we ensure it of our loyalty. Is it a paradox to undergo a collective benediction? A knife in the back of women's struggle? No. This is the precondition for a concrete emancipation, because it's either that or the perpetual divide, the "no-man's land" of the *beurette* or the disembodied black girl. From now on, this margin of freedom we negotiated will allow us to have a bit more control over our lives. It's significant and better than nothing. Within this framework, the "chocolate" dimension of feminism finds its fullest expression: the indigenous man is not our main enemy. The radical critique of indigenous patriarchy is a luxury. If a responsible form of feminism were ever to see the light of day, it would have to take the sinuous and craggy routes of a paradoxical movement, which will necessarily have to pass through a communitarian allegiance. At least, so long as racism exists.

Sisters, let's begin with an act of liberation. A simple thought. That of allowing ourselves to ask this question: must we necessarily subscribe to feminism? And why is this question, in and of itself, already an intolerable transgression? If so, does a new feminism need to be invented? For my part, I prefer to remain prudent and examine the matter more closely. We live in a complicated time, and this complexity makes our self-definition more difficult. Be that as it may, there is a need to clarify and to analyze in order to lead struggles that are adapted to our condition as non-white women of the East. For the purposes of our cause, I'm willing to use the concept of "decolonial feminism." Though it does not entirely satisfy me, it's a compromise between a certain resistance to feminism at home and throughout the Third World, and the massive, disturbing reality of the multidimensional violence that is inflicted on us, a violence that is produced by states and by neoliberalism.[13] Let's consider this compromise as an agreement between the resistance to feminism, to its Western-centric forms,[14] and its successful penetration into non-white worlds, its adoption and subsequent re-appropriation by some of us. It's a real mess. Let's start by clearing out a path.

Is feminism universal and atemporal, a necessary passage to aspire to liberation, dignity, and well-being? I don't think so. As is the case with all social phenomena, feminism is situated in space and time. One has only to determine its conditions of emergence. First, I must confess, I have a reproach to make against us: too often, feminists from the South see the feminist movement through Chimène's eyes. From the outset then, it's accepted as a superior phenomenon. This subjugation is such that Muslim feminists, for instance, do not hesitate to inscribe feminism within the genesis of Islamic history. All of Islam's dignity is thereby contained in the capacity of these militant women to prove that Islam's writings are feminist but its interpretations by the local patriarchy have been sexist. Muslim feminists are condemned to demonstrate this, and remain prisoners to the terms of a debate imposed by others. They sin through their blind adherence to the paradigm of modernity, through the idea that gender conflicts today are first and foremost determined by the nature of Islamic societies, rather than by global economic and political structures and North/South relationships. In this way, societies in which the feminist movement is nonexistent or marginal are seen as bearing a civilizational backwardness. One would have to make up this delay and operate grafts in different space/times, by ignoring the sociohistorical or even geopolitical realities of the countries in question, the impact of modernity in gender relations and their transformation, as well as the historical condition of the emergence of feminism, which have made feminism into a specifically European phenomenon, a phenomenon that emerges out of the geopolitical space called the West.

Sisters, let's be methodical and ask ourselves the right questions. Do white women really have an instinctive, feminist consciousness? What are the historical conditions that have *enabled* feminism? It's impossible not to relocate the basis of the *possibility* of feminism within a specific geopolitical moment: that of capitalist and colonial expansion, made possible by the "discovery of America" and by another foundational moment: the French Revolution, itself a condition of the emergence of the rule of law and of the individual citizen. The French Revolution became a promise—the promise of the recognition of complete and total universal citizenship—which was obviously not kept since this citizenship was at first reserved to men. It later became a possible horizon for women because, from then on, thanks to the principles of the revolution, they would be able to solve the equation: if the individual is a citizen, and woman is an individual, then woman is a citizen in full right…. Feminism would take a long time to develop (it reached its apogee in the 1970s) but would always be contained within the framework of liberal democracies, founded on the idea of the equality of citizens, and in which white women obtained rights, because of their own struggle, of course, but *also* thanks to imperial domination.

"The History of the West," writes Domenico Losurdo,

> faces a paradox […]. The neat line distinguishing white people on the one hand, from black people and Native Americans, on the other, favors the development of relationships of equality within the white community.[15]

Interesting, no? Let's not forget that at the time of the revolution, the black slave trade already existed and France was a stakeholder in this commerce. The "racial" conflicts of interest between the North and the South weren't fixed then. The peoples of the North who were not yet completely "white" could conceive of dangerous convergences with the colonized. The French Revolution coincides with the Haitian Revolution and interacts with it. The *sans-culottes* protested to demand the abolition of slavery against the "aristocracy of the epidermis." But the colonial states, in the process of being established, have always skillfully known how to integrate certain layers of the proletariat and of women throughout their social or political wings. This is also how the white race was invented. What I mean, sisters, is that European societies were horribly unjust toward women (several thousand "witches" were immolated there), but also that women, thanks to capitalist and colonial expansion, largely improved their condition on the backs of the colonized. So, let's stop dumbly admiring a world that birthed political phenomena only to resolve its own contradictions, be they justified or not, but which had nothing to do with an avant-garde enlightening of the world. Isn't this what James Baldwin and Audre Lorde invite us to do?

To Baldwin, who reproaches Lorde of overloading black men, the African American feminist replies:

> "I do not blame Black men; what I'm saying is, we have to take a new look at the ways in which we fight our joint oppression because if we don't, we're gonna be blowing each other up. We have to begin to redefine the terms of what woman is, what man is, how we relate to each other." Baldwin replies: "But that demands redefining the terms of the western world...."[16]

"But demands redefining the terms of the *western world*." Sisters, may I propose that we extend Baldwin's remark? The expansion of capitalism across the world exported political systems and conflicts that structure the white world into Left and Right, progressives and conservatives, nation states, languages, modes of life, dress codes, epistemologies, structure of thought…. There is no reason to believe that feminism escaped this. For me, feminism is indeed one of those exported European phenomena. The power of imperialism is such that all the phenomena that structure the Western political, economic, and cultural field impose themselves across the world more or less contentedly: sometimes they come up against the resistance of the people, sometimes they penetrate, slide in like butter. They become reality. They inform and shape the everyday. However, all these countries have specific histories, and they especially have specific economic and political systems that determine and shape, among other things, the relations between men and women. You might already know this, but before the "great encounter" with the West, there were places where relations of gender domination did not exist; there were even regions of the world in which the female gender did not exist.[17] There are regions where, on the contrary, there was a specifically local patriarchy, which is to say, not Christian-centric and not necessarily hetero-sexist. In fact, before the great colonial night, there was an extreme diversity of human relations that I do not want to romanticize, but that we cannot ignore. As Paola Bacchetta reminds us:

> The colonizers did not only impose their own notions of gender and sexuality onto colonized subjects: the effect of this imposition has been to worsen the situation of women [...] and sexual minorities.[18]

With fifty years of hindsight, and thanks to Latin American decolonizing intellectuals in particular, we know that while formal independence movements have indeed taken place, the "colonialism of power" has not disappeared. Indeed, the young liberated nations have walked in the footsteps of their old masters, copied their political systems without any critical distance, adopted the forms of European nation states, the French in particular, whose limits were painfully felt during the two so-called "world" wars, the forms of jurisdiction, of democracy, of relation to citizenship, to freedom, to emancipation.... The diversity of social forms thus gave way to a progressive homogenization. Diversity either disappeared or transformed itself. Often it resisted and reconstructed itself. This is what has happened in most cases. Feminism, as an idea, but also as a form of struggle, therefore sometimes becomes a reality that we must accept when women take hold of it and redefine it, whether it is secular, Islamic, or articulated through the local cultures, but that we should refuse, if women reject it.

This is what Baldwin suggests when he bases the redefinition of femininity and masculinity on a reconsideration of the West. He's completely right. We cannot rethink social relations, the family, gender relations, or sexuality without rethinking the nature of the state, North/South relations, neoliberalism, and its metamorphoses. Moreover, we must question the notions of equality, emancipation, freedom, and progress, and even refuse to conform to the liberal model of the individual.

Sisters, we need a global thinking that conceives of an alternative to Western civilization, which is in decline and has reached its limits. In other words, thinking about gender and the types of relations between men and women cannot be done without a radical calling into question of Modernity and a reflection on its civilizational alternative. It is not by targeting symptoms of masculine violence against us that we will transform our reality, but by attacking structures. In this struggle, our mobilization as non-white women will be decisive. But you will say, this is all well and good, and yet in the meantime, we are suffocating.

Yes.

To the question "why didn't you press charges," the black rape victim answers the interviewer, who is himself black:

> I never pressed charges because I wanted to protect you. I couldn't bear to see another black man in jail.[19]

This is what provokes Audre Lorde's rage.

> It's vital that we deal constantly with racism, and with white racism among black people—that we recognize this as a legitimate area of inquiry. We must also examine the ways that we have absorbed sexism and heterosexism. These are the norms in this dragon we have been born into—and we need to examine these distortions with the same kind of openness and dedication that we examine racism.

Our communities cannot do without this introspection. Men must learn to respect us and understand our sacrifice, just as we understand the necessity of protecting them.[20] This debate among ourselves is a priority. Will we see to it?

James Baldwin continues: "A woman does know much more than a man." Audre Lorde: "And why? For the same reason Black people know what white people are thinking: because we had to do it for our survival."

Yes, we know much more, and it is for this reason that we are more strategic...or sly, as others would say. We especially know that our men are just as oppressed as us in different ways.

"Do you know what happens to a man when he's ashamed of himself when he can't find a job? When his socks stink? When he can't protect anybody? When he can't do anything? Do you know what happens to a man when he can't face his children because he's ashamed of himself? It's not like being a woman...," says James Baldwin. And he continues:

> A Black man has a prick, they hack it off. A Black man is a ****** when he tries to be a model for his children and he tries to protect his women. That is a principle crime in this republic. And every Black man knows it. And every Black woman pays for it. And every Black child.

In Europe, prisons are brimming with black people and Arabs. Racial profiling almost only concerns men, who are the police's main target. It is to our eyes that they are diminished. And yet they try desperately to reconquer us, often through violence. In a society that is castrating, patriarchal, and racist (or subjected to imperialism), *to live is to live with virility.* "The cops are killing the men and the men are killing the women. I'm talking about rape. I'm talking about murder," says Audre Lorde. A decolonial feminism must take into account this masculine, indigenous "gender trouble" because the oppression of men reflects directly on us. Yes, we are subjected with full force to the humiliation that is done to them. Male castration, a consequence of racism, is a humiliation for which men make us pay a steep price. In other words, the more hegemonic thought tells us that our men are barbaric, the more frustrated they become, and the more they will oppress us. The effects of white, racist patriarchy exacerbate gender relations in the indigenous milieu. This is why a decolonial feminism must have as its imperative to radically refuse the discourses and practices that stigmatize our brothers and that, in the same move, exonerate white patriarchy. I think I can see that Lorde is conscious of this when she tells Baldwin:

> It's vital for me to be able to listen to you, to hear what it is that defined you and for you to listen to me, to hear what it is that defines me—because so long as we are operating in that old pattern, it doesn't serve anybody, and it certainly hasn't served us.

This has political and strategic implications. It means that we must engage with men in a conversation on masculinity, as the very lucid Baldwin invites us to do when he tells Lorde: "There's certainly not [a] standard of masculinity in this country which anybody can respect. Part of the horror of being a Black American is being trapped into being an imitation of an imitation."

The trap of imitation. Isn't this one of the many dimensions of the jihadist, Daesh phenomenon, that acts like a counter-revolutionary force? Isn't it into this trap that its promoters and fighters fall pray? The trap of grotesque imitation? The colonial West thought it had decimated the virile power of our men. Instead, the West proliferated it in its own image. Today, this power explodes in our faces, not without the active complicity of certain of our younger sisters, who were programmed to become *beurettes* but responded to the call of "jihad" with a resounding: yes! When their brothers go off to save their lost honor, they follow them, go with them, reinvent a mythological family model wherein the roles are naturalized but reassuring: men make war, women make children. The men are heroes and the women, loyal Penelopes who accept the downfall of a progressivism that was never shared, a falsely universal but truly white progressivism, which continues to try to domesticate them and hide their future from them: "No, our men aren't fags!" they tell us. We've come full circle.

In the face of this need for security, it will not suffice to implore or oppose great principles. If we had to have a mission, it would be to destroy imitation. This is a goldsmith's job. We will have to guess which part, in the testosterone-laden virility of the indigenous male, resists white domination. Then we will channel it, neutralize its violence against us, and orient it toward a project of common liberation. This fundamentally white masculinity will require something to offset it that is at least as gratifying. That is called respect. It's not complicated, but it's costly.

> I think the Black sense of male and female is much more sophisticated that the western idea.

Dear sisters, what do you think of this quote from brother Baldwin? I find it enigmatic because it seems misleading, given that our lived experiences contradict this affirmation. But I feel that it contains a knowledge that is hidden in our depths. It is full of a powerful potential, and even of a promise. I want to believe in it, but they will be quick to accuse me of giving in to an indigenous patriarchy. But after all, I don't care, because I'm decided on optimism and the triumph of revolutionary love.

5

WE, INDIGENOUS PEOPLE

> Songs a chance, France is right,
> we must give songs a chance,
> we must give songs a chance.
> — Charles Trenet

It is said that Josy Fanon suffered a severe trauma in October 1988, the day that the Algerian Army General Staff gave the order to shoot at the crowd of demonstrators. She cried out: "Poor Fanon, the Wretched have returned." She would commit suicide on July 13, 1989, a few days after Algerian Independence Day.

It is said that Marthe Moumié swore to have the remains of her deceased husband, Félix Moumié—the famous separatist who was assassinated by the French forces in Switzerland and buried in Guinea—repatriated to Cameroun. In Conakry, she met a cemetery guard who pointed her to some kind of coffin discarded in an alleyway, strewn directly on the ground, like detritus. The tomb had been desecrated. The activist, who dedicated her life to the independence of her country, fell apart. Moumié, did anyone even pray for you? Several years later, she would be raped and murdered by a band of thugs. Some say that the government wanted to liquidate a bad witness, others that it was nothing but a heinous crime. She would have been killed by children of the independence… for some cash.

It is said that Djamila Bouhired, the great Mujahida, who was adulated by all her people, no longer has the means to care for herself. The Algerian state, whose wallets abound and hold enough, allegedly, to pay off the French debt, does not take care of her. She would have written a letter in which she complained about this indignant treatment. Recently, the regime would have even allowed the destruction of the house of Larbi Ben M'hidi, one of the most illustrious martyrs of the Algerian Revolution, who was assassinated by Aussaresse. The maintenance of the house, which had become a site of pilgrimage, was too costly.

My heart breaks.

It is said that film archives dating from the colonial period showed French soldiers coldly executing indigenous people at point blank range. It is also said that in France, during the postcolonial period, reporters filmed the execution of a young guy from the suburbs who was trying to blow up a train, and live broadcast it for millions of viewers to see. His name was Khaled Kelkal.

I'm in pain.

It is said that more and more descendants of the colonized are tipping toward the banalization of Le Pen's extreme Right, which despises them with a passion and which has never condemned the use of torture in Algeria.

It is said that more and more of these immigrants' children want to shut down immigration for all migrants who come knocking on Europe's doors, because France can no longer "take in all the misery in the world."

It is also said that a handful of them take up arms to kill people blindly in café terraces or when school is let out, some of which are Jews, some of which are children.

I am suffocating. I feel like a sadistic hand is holding my head underwater and preventing me from catching my breath. The more I struggle, the more the hand applies pressure.

There is no longer any possible escape. We are part of the problem.

Wimps or monsters, servants or executioners, shoe-shiners or kamikazes. These are our only options. We have realized the white prophecy: to become non-beings or barbarians. Our complexities and our nuances have evaporated. We have been diluted, confiscated from ourselves, emptied out of all historical substance. We claim to be what we have been but are nothing but fantasmatic, disarticulated caricatures of ourselves. We cobble together disparate scraps of identity, held in place with bad glue. Our own parents look at us, perplexed. They think, "Who are you?"

Losers. My optimism will only be reborn on the threshold of this ultimate truth. *We are losers* perched on the charnel houses of our ancestors, powerlessly contemplating the industrial massacre of the Congolese, the Rwandans, the Syrians, and the Iraqis. *We are losers*. This, and this alone, will be my starting point. But this rebirth rejects all falsification. We are fugitives and we love the fables that prolong our flight. We hang on to glorious pasts. Pasts that we idealize and that artificially raise our self-esteem, so much so that we sometimes ape our masters and remain condemned to being nothing but pale copies. We are convincing neither in our cultural refinement nor in our crime. We seek the proof of ourselves in the past. We seek it in the mythical Andalusian-Arabic civilization, the only one capable of rivalling the supposed grandeur of Western civilization, when in fact we are nothing but the children of the *fellahs*,[1] who lived in the *douar*[2] of the Aures or Rif mountains. Or, we seek it in the pharaohs' Egypt. Hollywood made movies about Cleopatra, but not about Soundiata Keita, right? Those very pretentious Qatari skyscrapers, which rival New York's, are more gracious to our eyes than the ancestral skyscrapers of Sanaa in Yemen. And you really have to see it, this pathetic pride, when we brandish a verse from the Koran in which the atom is invoked. Because without the atom, there would be no atomic bomb, and without the atomic bomb, there would be no Hiroshima… *Hiroshima, mon amour*. Through us, this civilization of death becomes a plebiscite of everyday life.

I pity us! I don't have a manor or a castle. You don't either. I am neither a duchess nor a marquise. Neither are you. We have no noble titles. We aren't daddy's boys but we are our mothers and fathers' children. For the most part, they were workers, laborers, housewives, or cleaning ladies. They were born wretched of the earth, and they ended up immigrants. Immigrants since the very first exile, the one that sent them from the countryside to the city in their homelands, a consequence of colonialism, and the second, which sent them from their country to France, a consequence of colonialism. That's all. That's enough to make us major agents of France's history and of its present. And all the more so, now that we know precisely who we are and what we want. So, let's go back to our ancestors; it's more decent than telling each other stories that act like placebos and separate us from our destiny.

At the time, official discourse was clear about it. The immigration of workers was muscular. They were importing muscles to meet the needs of postwar reconstruction. In Europe, these muscles were busy rebuilding their own countries. Employers went looking for them in North Africa, in sub-Saharan Africa, and in the West Indies. The Right had no problem with this. The Left willingly admitted to this exploitation but was buying its time.

The voice: Let's not be too harsh on ourselves. Does France not also present an opportunity for the immigrant?

The immigrant would finally come to find the holy grail. He would be able to claim his rights. When he arrived in Marseille, the immigrant found himself face to face with democracy. He leaned over, and stumbled onto the rights of man, he turned to the right, bumped up against liberty. And when he turned left, he tripped over fraternity. He didn't know it yet but several decades later, he would have the ultimate encounter. The encounter with secularism, which would complete the integration of his spawn. Secularism played hard to get; it was hiding at the time. The immigrant shouldn't be too spoiled. He would not have known what to do with all these values at once. First he gave himself over to the taxation of sweat, to assembly-line labor, to working shifts, to the mine, the jackhammer. To prove his skills, to be fulfilled by this destiny ten hours a day, five days a week, for thirty or forty years. For, indeed, these French values are either inherited or earned. When he was most elegant, the immigrant knew how to let himself die before retirement.

Shut those chatterboxes up! It's the blues in our songs that tells the immigrant's story best.

"Oh plane, fly me away."[3]

"Oh plane, fly me away, toward Algeria, dear to my heart, Oh plane, fly me away, take me to my people. Oh plane, my heart is tormented, my nostalgia is all in flames. Take me to Algeria to amuse myself, and to visit Sidi Abderrahmane. In exile, I have found nothing but sorrow. Every day my suffering grows. Oh plane, take me to Oran, to visit the country of Sidi el Houari. Oh plane, exile is sad. Woe is he who is far away. Take me to Constantine, to visit the country of Sidi Rached. Oh plane, the exiled lives in servitude, while his country is luminous and happy. Take me for a stroll in the Kabylie mountains of Tizi Ouzou in Béjaïa. Oh plane, be tender with me. Understand the sorrows of exile. What a curse! Take me to Batna, to visit the Chaoui people, to Annaba and Sétif. Oh plane, fly me away, toward Algeria, dear to my heart, take me to my people.

"I am not from here."[4]

I am not from here; I am not from here. It is fate that has brought me here. I hope that the tortures of exile will have been worthwhile. A long flute, a long flute has wounded my heart and my soul. Distress lingers, I no longer sit in waiting for it to end. Melancholy, distress; I hope their days will run their course. If I had wings, I would fly away and come find you. If I had wings, wherever you were, I would go. My heart will heal; it is only close to you that I find peace. I am not from here; it is fate that has brought me here. Those of you who give in, you frustrate me. I want to visit my country and walk down every road. I am not from here. My country is far away. I am nostalgic; my heart is sad. I would be happy if I were surrounded by my own people.

"Oh France, oh France, what you have done with the people?"[5]

I left my country, free like a shooting star I went to the country of the impious, the country of obscurity.

I turn my tongue in my mouth seven times before I speak. They have neither pride, nor dignity and their women stroll freely and carelessly in the street. I inflict pain on myself because of this exile and I swear not to renew it. The Arab man is miserable there, he will never be worth anything, even if he is the colonel Bendaoued himself.

Oh France, oh France, what have you done with the people, what have you done with the people? You only like immigrants with picks and shovels in hand. When there was work, how they loved us with the dark-skin! They gave us dirty work, sewers and brooms. Oh France, Oh France, what have you done with the people? Now that there isn't any work to be found, they tell us it's over. Go back to your village. Oh France, Oh France, you only like Arabs with picks and shovels in hand. They sent the police and the CRS.[6] They said "get rid of the Arabs, be they immigrants or tourists." Oh France, Oh France, what have you done with the people? Now that there is unemployment, they despise us. They forgot about the factory, the leveling, and the mine. Oh France, Oh France, what have you done with the people? Slanderers laugh at us until they drool, the goat bleats and the donkey brays. Oh France, Oh France, what have you done with the people? The police arrive at the square. There is no longer any work, any traffic, any business.

"I eat bread and water."[7]

I eat bread and water but keep my head high. Oh my son, Oh my son, I love my country so. I can endure deprivation and hunger, but not humiliation. Oh my brothers, my sisters, Oh my brothers, my sisters, I am disgusted by the French. I can accept wearing nothing but a sweater but I do not want to be called a "bicot."[8] Oh God, my faith is better than theirs. Let the river carry away he who criticizes the homeland. Oh my country, Oh my country, no one will deceive me. I can accept having empty pockets but my dignity makes me their equal. El Houaria (Boumediene) teaches me. I work the twelfth and thirteenth month and the money comes in. I am a crafty Algerian. I eat bread and water but I always keep my head high. Oh my son, Oh my son, I love my country so.

"I am coming."[9]

No more bread for the Frenchman, no more space for the Arab. They came to an agreement against the dark-skinned. Apparently, they sent one back in a coffin, express delivery. I am coming, I am coming, make me tea. Paris and Marseille, it's over. Jaurès and Barbès, it's over. No more work, no more walks. The police and the CRS go hunting. I have neither the card nor the pay stub. I am coming, I am coming, make me tea. Paris and Marseille, Oh mother, it's over. All's well for the Frenchman in his office. But the Arab is a street sweeper. I've been slaving away for exactly twenty years in a foreign country. I lost everything to alcohol, I've been up to no good. I am coming, I am coming, make me tea. Paris and Marseille, Oh mother, it's over. The motherland is better than living abroad. There's no more poverty in the motherland. May Sétif, Bel Abbes, Tunis, and Meknes live on. Our Maghreb is still alive. No more bread for the Frenchman, no more space for the Arab. They came to an agreement against the dark-skinned. Apparently, they sent one back in a coffin, express delivery.

Exploitation, injustice, the colonial past, police crimes, humiliations, contempt, deracination, racism, "the colonized's racism," identity crises, nostalgia for and idealization of the homeland, Islam as refuge, troubled relationships to white women.[10] They're proliferating, those self-proclaimed experts, bazaar sociologists and two-cent anthropologists, who claim to have found the key to our mysteries in the interpretation of the Koran and in the folds of our supposedly fossilized customs, when in fact most of our secrets lie in our songs, right here, at arm's length, in these fragments of the immigrant memory. I remember that one day, my father told me he would never forget the family friend who pulled strings for him in the company to get him hired. I can't contradict my father, he who experienced hunger and deprivation. France was our saving grace, and the saving grace of our close family that stayed in Algeria, which my father fed for four decades with his pathetic salary. Algeria betrayed us. It offered us no prospects, despite our parents' dreams of going back there. This will be our eternal dilemma: to stay and suffer humiliation, or to leave and starve. But if asked, my father would have answered that he would always prefer his mother to France. It is also for her that he chose exile. She is dead, and he was separated from her by a sea and by her indigenous condition. He joined her prematurely, killed by his job. He left us, having made of us lifelong immigrants and profiteers.

"Houria, it's not because she is well dressed that she is clean." The teacher was giving us a lesson on appearances, teaching us that they were not to be trusted. I was in elementary school; I must have been eight years old. That day I learned that clothes don't make the white man. My teacher hit the nail on the head and I have never recovered—childhood determines one's homeland, doesn't it? My elders knew this and promised to avenge the insult. Several years later, we entered onto the big stage, all together, like princes.

I took my revenge.

We were five hundred at the beginning, but through quick reinforcement, we were one hundred thousand to arrive. It's 1983, the March for Equality and Against Racism. We descend upon Paris and impose ourselves for the first time onto the political scene. We would never leave. But who are they? Where were they hiding? Where do they come from? They asked in the salons, the magazines, the political organizations. From the slums, the *cités de transit*, the housing projects in Marseille, Lyon, Lille, and Paris.[11] "We aren't wild game for the cops." This was our rallying cry. Around our necks, already, we wore the Palestinian keffiyeh, in commemoration of the Sabra and Shatila massacre. It's a disaster for the socialist Left, which is trying to negotiate its liberal turn and which sees us, impetuous as we are, as a risk of reinforcement and radicalization of the extreme Left. Mitterand was preparing his great treason: the abandonment of the white proletariat in favor of social democracy. It is also a disaster for the pro-Israeli lobby, which must have experienced its first cold sweats. Up until the early 1980s, under the protective shield of the French Republic, Zionism was fit as a fiddle and led a happy life. Zionism would stroll around on the boulevards. Is Israel not a socialist project? Who are these cockroaches who have no complex vis-à-vis the Nazi genocide, no excuses, who don't even feign to be affected? Hundreds of thousands of *bicot* who escape the entire moral dispositif that frames white political correctness and determines the path of the spineless Left. A new phenomenon appeared: the emergence of an indigenous political body. The Shoah? The colonial subject has known tens of them. Exterminations? Galore. Torchings, raids? Tons. The indigenous person is not subject to manipulated emotions. After all, the independence movements are fresh, they are less than thirty years old.

The March for Equality "marks a rupture," writes Abdelmalek Sayad. It appears to be the first event since May '68, because it "brought immigration to political existence. And this political existence questions the Republic itself, which is constructed through the negation of indigenous political existence [...]. The mobilization of tens of thousands of indigenous peoples [...] shook up certain foundations of the Republican pact. The French nation, its cultural contours, its ethno-centric identity, its relationship to the world, the borders of citizenship that it has instated, which were struck by the colonized of the exterior thirty years earlier; all of this came crashing down with the irruption of the colonized of the interior onto the political stage in December 1983," explains Sadri Khiari.[12] As painful as it might have been for those who were skinned by the flag and for the syco-phants of an eternal, Gallic France, the message was clear: France will never again be as it was in Fernandel's films. Our presence on French soil Africanizes, Arabizes, Berberizes, Creolizes, Islamicizes, and blackens the eldest daughter of the Church, who was once white and immaculate, as surely as the waves' ebb and flow polishes and repolishes blocks of granite that aspire to eternity. We transform France. In other words, we partici-pate in the making of the identitarian norm, and through this, we call into question the republica-tion pact which is also a national-racial pact. We are becoming political agents. And our existence threatens the government in power. We didn't know this. But we were dangerous. Dangerous but also so harmless. Yes, harmless because amnesic. We have been intoxicated by our victories, the heroic independence movements, wrested at the cost of rivers of blood. That blood was worth free-dom for life, we thought. From that point on, we would *only* have to fight for equality. Today, this is laughable because we are beginning to understand that we are insoluble within white and Christian identity, but also because the egalitarian project is nothing but a project of integration that aims to make us French, "just like everyone else," within the imperialist nation. The page was turned too quickly, to the point of deracinating ourselves from our own history of struggle and from the Third World. "Every revolution is accompanied by a counter-revolution. This is nearly a rule of history."[13] Colonialism underwent a transformation, an adaptation, and continued to deploy its tentacles. New words emerged: "development aid," "humanitarian aid," "right of interference," "don't touch my friend".... We had barely begun to come to terms with our own victories when these words of soft ideology beguiled us. Had we only listened to the father of "Georgette":

"You're kidding, my girl... You don't know what's ahead of you! Listen to me and I'll tell you... There was a military man who had his father's name: Bendaoud. He was from a rich family. He finished his studies and entered the army; he became a colonel. One day, there was some trouble at work with a soldier named Lefrançois, his country's name. Both of them, on opposing sides, appeared before the military tribunal. And the tribunal ruled in favor of the soldier. The colonel couldn't believe it: how come he was proven wrong? Wasn't *he* the colonel?"

"And then what did he do?"

"He committed suicide... That's what happens, sweetheart, when you count on their word. That's what happens when you expect them to care about you."[14]

What "Georgette's" father is saying is what the West Indians have known for four centuries. They have been "French" for four hundred years. It only takes one generation for an Italian, a Portuguese, or a Pole to become *really* French, while this dignity will always in effect be denied to the old, deported Africans who remain relegated to the Hexagone or to dusty corners of the Empire—the Caribbean—as if they were forever in training. Too mixed-race, not white enough. What "Georgette's" father says is what the Harki and their children painfully experienced and continue to fight against up until this day. Whatever their allegiance to the French Algerian project might have been (whether voluntary or forced), the Harki never became French, a luxury which only Europeans can afford. History does not lie. The man of June 18 abandoned them and delivered them, disarmed, to the Algerian separatists. As for the metropolis, it parked them on reservations with their children. Too Arab to be French. Too indigenous to be white. What "Georgette's" father is saying is that if the Harki, who sacrificed themselves for the idea of France, didn't succeed in becoming white, and if their children, to this day, still haven't been "integrated," then what will become of us? What "Georgette's" father is saying is that between white people and us, there is race. It is constitutive of this Republic. It will always rise between us. If we were to escape it, it would not be against but with the children of the Harki. This presupposes that they identify the colonial Republic as their primary persecutor and that we do the same with regards to them. The Harki problem will never be an Algerian problem. It has a nationality. That of the General de Gaulle.

Brothers, do you remember that the leader of the March was the son a Harki? Yes? If so, let's go on.

The proponents of Black Power speak: "Powerlessness breeds a race of beggars."[15] This is what we are and will continue to be if we do not decide to stand up for ourselves, to think about power, and the strategy and means to attain it. We will be beggars so long as we do not break with our tutors, those who decide for us, without us, and against us. We will be beggars so long as we accept as universal the political divisions that cut up the white world and through which they conceive of the social conflicts and struggles that these divisions will engender. We will be beggars so long as we remain prisoners of their philosophy, of their aesthetic, and of their art. We will be beggars so long as we do not call into question their version of History. Let's accept rupture, discord, discordance. Let's ruin the landscape and announce a new era. Let's decide not to imitate them, to invent and draw from other sources. They say 1789. Let's answer 1492!

Let's adopt the point of view of the Native Americans. What do they say? Contrary to the white Lefts, which explain the world through what they call the capitalist expansion of Europe toward the Americas, Native Americans say that it is not only an economic system that came crashing down on them, but a globalism characterized by capital, colonial domination, the modern state, and the ethical system which accompanies it, which is to say, a religion, a culture, and a language. In other words, in 1492, what was imposed in the Americas was less an economic system than a civilization: Modernity.[16] They say: capitalist expansion therefore class struggle; we answer: colonial expansion therefore racial struggle.

Words. There are their words. And there are our words. Our words have magical qualities. They dehypnotize us and deliver to us venomous heritages.

"Indigenous." "White." "Social race." "White political field." "Colonialism of power." "Indigenous sovereignty." "Decolonial majority."

We who are engaged in the decolonizing struggle have never been so free as when these words came to find us. Ever since then, we have known who we are, what our position is, we know our weaknesses, we know our strengths. We are the *Indigenous of the Republic*. We rule over a political territory that we have conquered through infraction. Ever since then, we've provoked hatred, violence, fear, and respect. But never paternalism. Not a single person opens their mouth to talk to us about integration. And by intuition, one turns one's tongue in one's mouth seven times before speaking to us. Oh, there is still a certain crudeness ready to escape from an adventurous or ill-mannered mouth. But in our presence, prejudices and paternalism keep a low profile. When we come closer, they move away. To declare oneself indigenous is a victory against the *indigénat*.[17] But it is first and foremost a victory against the self and against one's own narcissism. Did Malcom not reject the name "Little" in order to substitute it with that of "X," proof of his uncompromising lucidity? Laziness—or comfort—make us prefer "Black is beautiful!" Why not? But why not do away with this step altogether? Others have done it before us, others have done it *for us*. All these flowers on the ground, let's pick them. Of course black, Arab, Muslim, Roma is beautiful. This is a step of our awareness, but "black is—first and foremost—political." As is "indigenous." These are words that mean: "We no longer want to play *your* game. From now on, we will play *our own*."

But this game will be political or it will not be.

We are the *indigènes de la République*, in France, in Europe, in the West. To the Third World, we are white. Whiteness is not a genetic question. It is a matter of power. Already, the brothers whom we abandoned over there look at us with an oblique eye. We won't be able to hide from our responsibilities for much longer. We must accept our role in the crime. In euphemistic terms, our integration. Of course, our history, our attachments, make us more sensitive to the Third World's cause, more spontaneous, especially because our lot here depends on that of the peoples of the South to whom we have been assimilated. But a part of ourselves has become bourgeois, protecting its little, indigenous, aristocratic privileges against the flea-ridden "villagers" who force the doors of Europe, embarrassing us. We are complicit in the exploitation of the South. Luckily, under these skies, we are not beloved. There is no future here for the "Bendaoued colonels." What if we took advantage of racism to invent new political horizons? What if we took advantage of the "failure of integration"? Dare-I say that we must even draw some satisfaction from it? Our oppressors' territory is itself shifting. When the nation had been bled dry, they invent Europe, and when Europe itself is bled dry, they seek refuge in white Christianity, which acts as a political geography and stretches all the way to the United States and Australia. If there was ever a time to imitate white people, it's now or never. To spread far beyond the borders of the Nation, to go in search of our solidarities in England, in the United States, in Portugal, or in

Australia. Because together with the colonial sub-
jects of colonial metropolises, we form this group
of the wretched of the interior, at once victims
and exploiters. It would be inappropriate to con-
fuse us with the great South because there is,
objectively, a conflict of interest between us and
them, if only because of the partial redistribution
of the pillaging, and because our lives are more
protected, because foreign armies do not rule the
roost here, and because we do not have bombs
falling on our heads. I don't have any lessons to
give them, but the people of the South must stop
looking toward the North and start privileging
South-South alliances. While it is true that the
conflicts of interest, the fractures and divisions
(between nation states, ethnicities, religions, gen-
ders, colors) are numerous there, the majority of
the population in the South is united by similar
conditions. They undergo a double violence: the
military, political, economic, and cultural violence
of the West, and the authoritarian and dictatorial
violence of their own rulers. As for us, we form a
historical and social unity in the North. All we
have left to do is to turn it into a political unity.

But, it may be said, once this unity is broken,
one can imagine that the colonized people
might be able to reconstitute it and integrate
its new experiences, hence its new wealth, with

the framework of a new unity, a unity that will no longer be the old unity, but a unity nevertheless.[18]

To reconnect with Bandung and create a kind of Tricontinent within the West? I can already see them laughing and talking about a fifth column. Let's leave them to their sarcasm and concentrate on our horizon. Who better than us to be proactive? Who better than us to compel, through a game of power relations, antiracist and anti-imperialist white people to fight the imperialist and neoliberal politics of their country, to help decolonize their organizations, and give up on dictating the best way to fight? Who better than us to create the conditions of possibility for great alliances between the Third World people in the West and the white proletariat, to resist the Third-Worldization of Europe? The entirety of this process could be related to *an international division of activist labor*: on a national scale, a domestic internationalism, and on an international scale, a decolonizing internationalism, to contain the devastating effects of the crisis of capitalism, which is also a civilizational crisis, and to participate in the transition toward a more human model.

To get there, we will have to dismantle our instinctive ideology: integrationism.

Every young American black who writes is trying to find himself and test himself and sometimes, at the very center of his being, in his own heart, discovers a white man he must annihilate.[19]

This is a white brother speaking. Jean Genet. He's right, but why is he saying this? Is it out of pure philanthropy? Let's listen to him carefully. He is beseeching us. He is asking for help. To annihilate the white man at the center of our own being is to annihilate the white man at the center of his own being. He knows that we are the only ones who can get rid of it. As the proponents of Black Power already noted:

We are now faced with a situation where conscienceless power meets powerless conscience, threatening the very foundations of our nation.[20]

The madness of Westerners will eventually turn against them—in the form of economic or terrorist violence. The great experts of the Europe of markets did not hesitate to dismiss Greece like one dismisses a vulgar servant. With disconcerting tranquility, they initiated the Third-Worldization of what they consider to be the cradle of their civilization and, through this, of all of Europe. Our (civilizing?) mission will not be achieved if we fail to heed Genet's call. To annihilate the white man at the center of our being, is to free him, to prepare for the "*Great Replacement*." Human rather than white, Human rather than black. The dignity of Genet is at stake. Will we hear his plea?

But what should we offer to white people in exchange for the "salary of whiteness"? This is an open question, to which Genet only partially responds. He knew that he was freed through our struggle, but most white people, who will strategize based on very short term calculations, will feel threatened. Unfortunately for us, the development of a decolonial force will reinforce the most racist and reactionary fringes. They will even be galvanized. Nationalist forces will find in this the confirmation of their phantasms and instrumentalize us to reinforce white resistance, by surfing on fear and the vivacious and ever-ready colonial imaginary. We will have to anticipate this moment, for, the rest of the white political field to which our allies belong will deploy all of its forces to intimidate us. They will say: "You play the same game as the FN. You will have to bear the responsibility of its electoral progress." This blackmailing will be permanent, but we will have to hold steady and answer, unscrupulously: "You play the same game as the FN if you do not, once and for all, turn your attention toward working class neighborhoods and immigration. You will bear the responsibility of the extreme Right's advances. We will not make any concessions. It will be heaven or hell for all." We will then walk on a tightrope, for the threat will be real. Will our action reinforce the white political field or, on the contrary, will we succeed in breaking it and building a decolonizing majority? It is up to us to find the most convincing "offer." It must contain at least one promise: peace. Surely, the most precious good. But will they be aware enough to make this their primary political objective? This is a wager. If they persist in tampering with this word, in corrupting it and abandoning it in the swamps of bad faith or good conscience, then they will be responsible for everything that will happen to them, for as we all know: no justice, no peace. It's a two-person game, and if we are not united in victory, we will be united in defeat.

A memory is coming back to me now, a memory told by Fatima Ouassak:

> My mother, with much hindsight and humor, would tell me that when she took me to school, I would try to remove my hand from hers, for as the school and the teacher came into view, she could tell I was ashamed of her, of her garishly-colored clothes, of her scarf, of her Arab-tinted French… And she would hold my hand even tighter until we reached our destination, sometimes even going so far as to speak to the teacher.[21]

DIGNITY. This word, dignity, I don't know how to define it, exactly. But I know it when I see it. It's in this relationship between a mother and her child and in the fluid that allowed the daughter to draw from it an education and learn to look white people in the face. It is conscious of itself and conscious of the other, of the finitude of these two, antagonistic poles, which will be reconciled in death.

Dignity is in our ability to distinguish stars from sequins. All this artifice that white people saddle themselves with to maintain a distance and subjugate us. It is in Zhou Enlai's[22] implacable retort when a French journalist asked him: "In your opinion, what is the impact of the French Revolution?" The cruel response of someone who knows how to recognize the stars: "It's too early to tell."

Dignity is to know that you are responsible for one, for ten, for a thousand people. It is our capacity to love ourselves and to love that Other— that irresponsible one—to prevent him from deploying his madness even more and, with him, to save what is left to salvage of this poor world.

Dignity, who better to say it than Malcom X?

I love everybody who loves me. But I sure don't love those who don't love me.

Dignity? It's as simple as revolutionary love. There, our wings give us a push, and we fly away.

ALLAHOU AKBAR!

"God is dead, Marx is dead, and I don't feel too well myself."

—Woody Allen

"Allah is beautiful and love what is beautiful."[1]

"There is no god but God."[2]

"There are stars in the sky that have been extinguished, never to light up again."[3] There were humans who boasted of this crime. Of the disenchantment of the world and of their conflict with the Church—from which they draw a universal truth—the French are rather proud. They killed God, decreed the end of History, and praised Reason, which they call "human" out of false modesty but believe is ontologically French. Because the French Revolution is

the mother of all modern revolutions. It prefigures the Republic as it rises against the monarchic order; it offers the Declaration of the Rights of Man to humanity, and consecrates its universal character. The French Revolution announces the secularization of society, which will become a hyper-secularization (through the combination of anticlericalism, surely justified within the context of the time, capitalism, and the reason of the State). It draws a *tabula rasa* of all transcendence, to the point where secularism ends up being confused with collective impiety and the state's neutrality with atheism—which is, nevertheless, a belief like any other. Therefore, when a white Frenchman crosses paths with a Muslim Frenchman, he does not encounter a friend or an enemy, but rather, an enigma. Who is this human who persists in prostrating himself five times a day in degrading positions, fasts for a month in often sweltering weather, protects his body and hair from leering eyes, and contributes month after month, year after year, to a fund to build a mosque in the city where his children will grow up, rather than transfer his offerings to the Restos du Cœur?[4] Who is this foolish creature to whom we have delivered Enlightenment on a silver platter, and who persists in turning toward Mecca, like a sunflower that only the sun can subjugate?

This creature knows something that escapes white Reason. Instinctually, because he too recognizes the stars, he has no confidence in the myth of Modernity, which makes promises that it does not keep. His scars, once blessed by the colonies, are still bleeding. He knows better than anyone else the fragility of the modern and the solidity of the archaic. And when he invests, he does not mobilize abstractly universal reason, but his own, which proceeds from his experience and his condition.

We are experiencing a negative moment. Everything appears to be dying. It is the end of the great narratives and emancipatory projects. More than a crisis of perspective, we are witnessing a moral collapse, a crisis of meaning, a crisis of civilization that is conflated with a crisis of Western conscience. And more and more, this crisis looks like suicide. To the stagnation and disappearance of political utopias and of all kinds of "civil religions" (that can take the place of the religious when it becomes scarce), the indigenous person opposes his own rationality. Ashis Nandy shares this hypothesis:

> Why should we adopt the priorities and the hierarchies of the West? Are your 20th century successes so brilliant? World War Two, genocides, the destruction of the environment, what's next? Here are the effects of a "modern" civilization which has privileged the individual over metaphysics, History over

eternity, progress over tradition, manly values over sensitivity.[5]

Many many decades later, in the aftermath of that marvel of modern technology called the Second World War and perhaps that modern encounter of cultures called Vietnam, it has become obvious that the drive for mastery over men is not merely a byproduct of a faulty political economy but also of a world view which believes in the absolute superiority of the human over the nonhuman and the subhuman, the masculine over the feminine, the adult over the child, the historical over the ahistorical, and the modern or progressive over the traditional or the savage. It has become more and more apparent that genocides, ecodisasters and ethnocides are but the underside of corrupt sciences and psychopathic technologies wedded to new secular hierarchies, which have reduced major civilizations to the status of a set of empty rituals. The ancient forces of human greed and violence, one recognizes, have merely found a new legitimacy in anthropocentric doctrines of secular salvation, in the ideologies of progress, normality and hypermasculinity, and in theories of cumulative growth of science and technology.[6]

I have often heard this phrase, "the immigrant is an opportunity for France," spoken by humanists who, against the extreme Right, try to demonstrate—rather in vain—the utility of the immigrant. This "utility" is more often than not economic. The immigrant pays taxes, consumes in France and creates riches. Well, what if there was another kind of utility? That, for instance, of carrying with him and conserving the memory of societies based on solidarity, where collective consciousness is strong and where each and every person feels responsible for the group as a whole. Or that of resisting the atomization of society and fanatical individualism. That of protecting the individual against bare life, instead of this "to each his own." Everything will have been said about Islam and "communitarianism" except for this blindingly obvious fact, which is nevertheless Islam's foundation. Our wise men say: "May God protect us from the word I." The immigrant faithfully did what he could to preserve the ultimate meaning of this saying in a France that exalts the liberal, consumer, pleasure-seeking "I." An "I" that motivates the market and crushes every indecisive "we," starting with the postcolonial "we," which is opportunistically stigmatized as tribal. Unlike the bourgeois, arrogant, and cynical elite of this country, the immigrant knows the white proles. He knows them. He knows how they were delivered—disarmed, without God, communism, or any social horizon—to big business. That painful gaze which accompanies the disintegration of his family, his solidarities, and his hopes, time and time again—the immigrant met it. It is even possible that he could have read in it, at times, a sad confession. "At least you have something left to hold on to." Yes. From his faith, the indigenous person draws his power. The immigrant is a political man who does not know himself. He is a guide. His intuitions are powerful and his survival instinct is sharp. To the mirages of a civilization that birthed the nuclear man, in both senses of the word, where he is located and where he has been assigned—the place of the radical Other—and to he who claims to challenge God, the immigrant answers: *Allahou akbar!*

And he adds: *There is no god but God.* In Islam, divine transcendence calls for humility and the permanent awareness of the ephemeral. Are not the wishes, the projects of his followers all punctuated by the phrase "in cha Allah"[7]? We begin one day and end another. Only the Almighty is eternal. No one can challenge his power. Only the vain believe they can. From this complex of vanity are born blasphemous theories on the superiority of white people over non-white people, on the superiority of men over women, on the superiority of humans over animals and nature. There is no need to be a believer to interpret this philosophy from a profane point of view. Faithful or not, it's a wisdom that is completely "rational" and can be supported by all. Right when this vanity reaches its paroxysmal point, when the nuclear man has exhausted the earth, asphyxiated the air, and polluted the seas, right when nature takes its revenge on this mistreatment, there are victims of this ruthless order to call him back to the world: *Allahou akbar!* At last—a universal point of view—understood by other "radical Others," the Native American Hopi tribe:

> And the path of the Great Spirit has become difficult to see by almost all men, even by many Indians, who have chosen instead to follow the path of the white man.... Today, the sacred lands where the Hopi live are being desecrated by men who seek coal and water from our soil that they may create more power to the white man's cities. This must not be allowed to continue, for if it does, Mother Nature will react in such a way that almost all men will suffer the end of life as they now know it.[8]

But this cry—*Allahou akbar!*—terrorizes the vain, who see in it a project of decline. They are right to fear it, for its egalitarian potential is real: to put men, all men, back in their place, without any form of hierarchy. Only one entity is allowed to rule: God. No other entity is granted this power to exercise against one's peers or against God. Thus, white people take their place alongside all their brothers and sisters in humanity: the place of simple mortals. We might call this a utopia, and it is one. But to re-enchant the world will be a difficult task. For to absorb the misery, to respond to the despair and the collapse of ideals is a burden too great for a "Third peoples" that is weakened, precarious, and unorganized. To re-enchant the world is a challenge too great for a community that, short of solving the economic crisis, limits its damage by attempting to solve the crisis of meaning. The bet is partly won. Few people know this but Islam has saved more than one soul—from prison, from drugs, from suicide—and has guided more than one on the path to resistance. Respect. But there is still much work to be done and all other liberation utopias will be welcome, wherever they may come from, be they spiritual or political, religious, agnostic, or cultural, so long as they respect Nature and the human being, who is fundamentally only one element among all others.

If the social impasses, the clouded horizons, together with the desecration of the social universe, plunge part of the white youth into movements that exacerbate European and Christian nationalisms, a small part of the youth from the projects, for its part, damages itself in a bellicose romanticism, in which authoritarianism and sacrifice are exalted in the name of a cause whose horizon is apocalyptic. This takes place at the expense of a political vision that conceives of systems and does not give up on complexity. A thought in which the "West" is a historical category and never an essence. The same goes for human groups forming a humanity whose choices, in context, are dialectical and shifting. Yet, groups seeking plenitude and absolute truth have this in common that they invent imaginary enemies for themselves (that are often defined social groups) and rarely systems. In this infra-political universe, they are the heroes of an intoxicating epic, rather than the respected citizens they dream of being and the indigenous people they refuse to remain. This is the marginal but significant product of a progressive de-politicization of the youth from the projects, programed by social democracy. At the end of this logic, monsters appear. Fifty years ago, James Baldwin already worried about this.

> What will come of all this beauty? For Blacks, even though some of us, Blacks and White, do not see it yet, are very beautiful. And when seated at Elijah's table [...] we spoke of the vengeance of God—or Allah—I wondered: and when this vengeance is consumed, what then will come of all this beauty? I also felt that the intransigence and the ignorance of the white world might make this vengeance

inevitable, [...] a historical vengeance, a cosmic one, founded on the law, which we recognize when we say: "Everything that goes up must come down.[9]

Malcom X, who became Malek El-Shabazz, was killed because he was beautiful.

"I have never hated anyone." These words in his mouth drop like a bomb. The newspapers wrote that the bard of Black Pride no longer hated white people. But doubt remains. I smile with lassitude. The American media projected their own pathos onto him. And yet, black literature is there to educate and cure them. Why don't they prostrate themselves to gather what so many generations of African Americans have given them in poetry and spirituality?

We spoke of the Whites. "They're God's children, just like us," he said. "Even if they don't act very godlike anymore. God tells us straight—we've got to love them, no *ifs*, *ands*, and *buts*. Why, if we hated them, we'd be sunk down to their level..." [...] "You can't get around what's right, though," he said. "When we stop loving them, that's when they win."

"How's that?"

"Then they'll have ruined our race for sure.

They'll have dragged us down plumb to the bottom."[10]

Malcom X was therefore killed because he was beautiful. He refused the destruction of his race. The idea that Malcom could have hated white people is despicable. Malcom does not lie. He has no reason to lie. Hatred would have fatally tipped him over into the world of white people. Is this a life's ambition? To imitate one's enemy. To hate. Are the media serious when they accuse him of being nothing but the inverse reflection of what they are? Are they blind? Are they not moved by his beauty? Malcom does not hate white people. He hates white power. This is why he spent his short life *lowering everything that rises*. For what are these white people doing above his head, wiping themselves on him, walking all over him, when their destiny, as taught in the Bible, their own Book, is to *return to ashes*?

Malcom is a moment. He is a time. He is that moment right before hatred. He anticipates it. Like Baldwin, he fears for the beauty of black people. Is racial hatred not a white sentiment? Are we ready to sell off our beauty? Will we capsize? He fears vengeance but he knows that when the moment comes, he won't condemn it. Didn't he dedicate half of his life to forewarning? Does he love white people? No, they don't deserve his love, but he creates the condition of its possibility. He did this up until the day of his death. He tried to *lower everything that rises*. Vengeance or revolution? He answers: revolution. Malcom is assassinated during a meeting. He died fighting. Malcom X is a sun. His beauty shines. It irradiates us. Black is so beautiful when the struggle consists in lowering all those who commit the sacrilege of raising themselves to God's level.

Beauty, poetry, spirituality—this is what is most cruelly lacking from our modern, dry, societies.

White people know perfectly well that their society is dry. They know that they are egotistical and individualistic. And they suffer from it. But they lack the imagination to think up other horizons. Because they have lost their memory. They have forgotten what they were before being engulfed by modernity. They no longer remember the time when they stood in solidarity and when there were still cultures, chants, regional languages, and traditions. For us, it's a bit different. In the face of adversity, we preserve this memory. This is where our attachment to family and community comes from. But, like them, we are sucked up in it. And soon, like them, we will replace the word "solidarity" with that of "tolerance" and all those bloodcurdling, terrifying words. The dissolution of our identities attests to this. Not so long ago, we knew how to define an African, an Algerian, a

Muslim. We held strong opinions. Today, every-thing is muddled. What does "African" mean when the continent stands by, helpless, as its intellectuals set off for other shores? What does "Algerian" mean after a civil war that killed over 200,000 people? What does "Muslim" mean when Mecca is under the tutelage of the Saudis and Islam is threatened by Macdonaldization? What does "French" mean when the population is dispossessed of its sovereignty for the benefit of the rich and powerful? What does "European" mean when the people of Europe did not lift a finger to save Greece?

And as for me, who am I? I know neither how to make my mother's *kesra*,[11] nor her *makroud*. The *kesra* that our grandmothers prepared clandes-tinely, risking their lives, to feed the freedom fighters; the *kesra* that fed two generations of immigrant workers; the *kesra* that never left the *ftour* table during Ramadan, and thanks to which we knew we were different. Different from those who ate baguette, but with whom we would gladly share it? What I am? I know… I am a modern and integrated woman who does not know how to make *kesra* and who was taught to be proud of betraying her mother.

But, enough of the tears and regrets. The past is no longer. We are the sum of our acts of cowardice and resistance. We will be what we deserved to be.

That's all. This is true for all of us, black or white. This is where the question of the great WE will be raised. The We of our encounter, the We of the surpassing of race and its abolition, the We of a new political identity that we will have to invent together, the We of a decolonizing majority. The We of the diversity of our beliefs, our convictions, and our identities, the We of their complementarity and their irreducibility. The We of this peace that we will have earned because of the high price it cost us. The We of a politics of love, which will never be a politics of the heart. For to produce this love, there is no need to love or feel sorry for one-self. One will have only to recognize the other and embody that moment "right before hatred" to push it back as much as possible and, with the energy of despair, to dispel the worse. This will be the We of revolutionary love.

So, let's start at the beginning. Let's repeat as often as necessary: *Allahou akbar!* Let's détourn Descartes and *lower everything that rises.*

I think therefore I am, I am…a *khoroto*. That will do for my gravestone.

Notes

1. Shoot Sartre!

1. Jean-Paul Sartre, "Conversations with Jean-Paul Sartre," in Simone de Beauvoir, *Adieux: A Farewell to Sartre*, trans. Patrick O'Brian (Harmondsworth: Penguin, 1985), 378, 367.

2. White militants who provided material aid to the Algerian FLN, particularly by carrying suitcases full of bills or weapons.

3. Translator's note: Front de Libération National [Algerian National Liberation Front].

4. Jean-Paul Sartre, preface to *The Wretched of the Earth*, by Frantz Fanon, trans. Richard Philcox (New York: Grove Press, Inc. 2004), lv.

5. Jean-Paul Sartre, "About Munich," trans. Elizabeth Bowman, *Sartre Studies International*, 9 (2003): 7–8.

6. Jean-Paul Sartre, "Un émouvant appel de J.-P. Sartre en faveur de la Palestine libre," *L'Ordre de Paris* (April 7, 1948), reprinted as "C'est pour nous tous que sonne le glas" [The Bell Tolls for All of Us], *Caliban*, 16 (1948): 15. Translation mine.

7. See Simone de Beauvoir, *Force of Circumstance*, trans. Richard Howard (London: Weidenfeld & Nicolson, 1966).

8. Sartre, "Un émouvant appel," 15. Translation mine.

9. Madeleine Jacob, "Le problème juif? Un problème international, déclare J.-P. Sartre au procès des amis du Stern" *Franc-Tireur*,

February 14, 1948. Cited in Noureddine Lamouchi, *Jean-Paul Sartre et le tiers-monde: rhétorique d'un discours anticolonialiste* (Paris: L'Harmattan, 1996). Translation mine.

10. "Palestinian state" used to mean "Israel" at the time.

11. Jean-Paul Sartre, "The Birth of Israel," trans. Mitch Abidor, https://www.marxists.org/reference/archive/sartre/1949/israel.htm, originally published in *Hillel* 7 (1949): 6, reprinted in Michael Contat and Michel Rybalka, eds. *Les Écrits de Sartre* (Paris: Gallimard, 1970), 212.

12. Jean-Paul Sartre, *Anti-Semite and Jew: An Exploration of the Etiology of Hate*, trans. George J. Becker (New York: Schocken Books, 1944), 49.

13. Jean-Paul Sartre, "Pour la vérité," *Les Temps Modernes*, no. 253 bis (June 1967): 5–11.

14. Josie Fanon, "À propos de Frantz Fanon, Sartre, le racisme et les Arabes," in Lamouchi, *Jean-Paul Sartre et le tiers-monde*, 157–58. Originally published in *El Moujahid*, June 10, 1967. Translation mine.

15. *Le Nouvel Observateur* (November 17–22, 1975).

16. Jean Genet, "Interview with Bertrand Poirot-Delpech," in *The Declared Enemy: Texts and Interviews* (Stanford, CA: Stanford University Press, 2004), 203.

17. Genet, "Interview with Bertrand Poirot-Delpech," 194.

18. As Bertrand Poirot-Delpech called him.

19. Both quotes Genet, "Interview with Bertrand Poirot-Delpech," 200.

20. Sylvie Rosier, "L'héritage d'Aimé Césaire," *Le Monde des lecteurs*, February 17, 2012, http://mediateur.blog.lemonde.fr/2012/02/17/lheritage-daime-cesaire/.

21. Aimé Césaire, *Discourse on Colonialism*, trans. Joan Pinkham (New York: Monthly Review Press, 1972), 18.

22. Césaire, *Discourse on Colonialism*, 14.

23. Translator's note: from Ancient Greece, where the term *metic* referred to a foreign resident of Athens who did not have citizen rights in their Greek city-state of residence. Today, the term *métèque* has been used pejoratively against primarily Mediterranean immigrants and foreigners living in France.

24. Translator's note: the *Indigenous of the Republic* is the name of an open call published in January 2005, which gave way to the founding of an organization, a political movement, the Movement of the Indigenous of the Republic (le "Mouvement des indigènes de la République") and a political party, the Party of the Indigenous of the Republic (le "Parti des indigènes de la République") for which Houria Bouteldja is currently a spokesperson. See the PIR's website: http://indigenes-republique.fr/. A translation of the open call is available at: http://decolonialtranslation.com/english/AppelEng.php

25. The date of the conquest of Algeria.

26. Antonio Gramsci, "Wave of Materialism" and "Crisis of Authority" [1930], *Selections from the Prison Notebooks*, eds. and trans. Quintin Hoare and Geoffrey Nowell-Smith (New York: International Publishers, 1971), 276.

27. Nicolas Sarkozy, "Discours de Dakar" [Dakar Speech] University of Cheikh-Anta-Diop, Dakar, Senegal, July 26, 2007. See https://fr.wikipedia.org/wiki/Discours_de_Dakar.

28. "Claude Guéant persiste et réaffirme que 'toutes les cultures ne se valent pas" [Claude Guéant persists and reaffirms that 'not all civilizations are equal'], Le Monde (February 5, 2012), http://www.lemonde.fr/election-presidentielle-2012/article/2012/02/05/claude-gueant-declenche-une-nouvelle-polemique_1639076_1471069.html

29. Antoine Lerougetel, "France: Une nouvelle loi oblige les enseignants à presenter le 'rôle positif' de la colonisation française" [France: A new law forces teachers to present the 'positive impact' of French colonization"], World Socialist Web Site, December 19,

2005, https://www.wsws.org/francais/News/2005/Decembre05/
201205_colonialismeEcole.shtml

30. Sadri Khiari, *Pour une politique de la racaille: immigré-e-s,
indigènes et jeunes de banlieues* (Paris: Textuel, 2006), 152.
Translation mine.

2. You, White People

1. Quino, *Mafalda* (Grenoble: Glénat, 2014), Bande 1766.
Translation mine.

2. René Descartes, *Discourse on Method* [1637], trans. Donald A.
Cress, 3rd ed. (Indianapolis, IN: Hackett Publishing Company,
1998), 35.

3. This refers to Malek Bennabi's concept of "colonizability." See
Bennabi, *Islam in History and Society*, trans. Asma Rashid
(Islamabad, Pakistan: Islamic Research Institute, International
Islamic University, 1988), originally published as *Vocation de
l'Islam* (Paris: Éditions du Seuil, 1954).

4. Charles Baudelaire, "Reversibility," in *The Flowers of Evil*, ed.
Marthiel and Jackson Mathews, trans. Frank Pearce Sturm (New
York: New Directions, 1989), 56.

5. Fanon, *The Wretched of the Earth*, 50.

6. Césaire, *Discourse on Colonialism*, 10.

7. James Baldwin, "C'est dur d'être un blanc!" Interview with
James Baldwin by Hervé Prudon, *The Nouvel Observateur* (April
29, 1983): 94. Translation mine.

8. "Immune System," *Wikipedia*, last modified January 2, 2017,
https://en.wikipedia.org/wiki/Immune_system. Originally from
the French, "Système immunitaire," *Wikipedia*, last modified
November 17, 2016, https://fr.wikipedia.org/wiki/Syst%C3%
A8me_immunitaire.

9. "Système immunitaire," *Avène lexicon*, accessed January 2, 2017,
http://www.eau-thermale-avene.fr/lexique/definition-systeme-
immunitaire

10. Richard Wright, quoted in Jean-Paul Sartre, *Anti-Semite and Jew: An Exploration of the Etiology of Hate*, trans. George J. Becker (New York: Schocken Books, 1976), 109. Originally published as Richard Wright, quoted in Maurice Nadeau, "There's No Black Problem in the U.S.A., but a White Problem, the Black Writer Richard Wright Tells Us," trans. Keneth Kinnamon, *Combat* (May 11, 1946): 1, reprinted in *Conversations with Richard Wright*, eds. Keneth Kinnamon and Michel Fabre (Jackson: University Press of Mississippi, 1993), 88.

11. Genet, "Interview with Bertrand Poirot-Delpech," 204.

12. Sadri Khiari, *La contre-révolution coloniale en France: De de Gaulle à Sarkozy* (Paris: La Fabrique, 2009).

13. Sadri Khiari, "Internationalisme décolonial, antiracisme et anticapitalisme" (lecture presented at "Penser l'émancipation conference, University of Lausanne, Switzerland, October 25, 2012), http://indigenes-republique.fr/internationalisme-decolonial-antiracisme-et-anticapitalisme.

14. C. L. R. James, "The Making of the Caribbean People," in *Spheres of Existence: Selected Writings* (London: Allison and Busby, 1980), 187.

15. James Baldwin, *The Fire Next Time*, 2nd ed. (New York: Vintage, 1992), 102.

3. You, the Jews

1. Translator's note: in the North African context, an isolated, usually rural region, where people live or come from (if they have immigrated). In French, it is used to describe a little village, usually pejoratively: the middle of nowhere.

2. Sartre, *Anti-Semite and Jew*, 70.

3. George Perec, "Ellis Island: Description d'un projet," in *Je suis né* (Paris: Édition du Seuil, 1990), 99. Translation mine.

4. Jules Renard, "October 29, 1897," in *Journal 1893–1898*, http://www.atramenta.net/lire/journal-de-jules-renard-de-1893-1898/4380. Translation mine.

5. Bertold Brecht, *The Resistible Rise of Arturo Ui*, trans. Ralph Mannheim (New York: Arcade Publishing, 1981).

6. Césaire, *Discourse on Colonialism*, 14.

7. Ibid., 17.

8. See Enzo Traverso, "Memory: The Civil Religion of the Holocaust," *The End of Jewish Modernity*, trans. David Fernbach (London: Pluto Press, 2016), 113–127.

9. Claude Lanzmann, preface to Carles Torner, *Shoah, une pédagogie de la mémoire* (Paris: Éditions de l'Atelier, 2001), 130. Translation mine.

10. Rosa Luxembourg, *The Letters of Rosa Luxembourg*, eds. Georg Adler, Peter Hudis, and Annelies Laschitza, trans. George Shriver (London: Verso, 2011), 376. Quoted in Traverso, *The End of Jewish Modernity*, 32.

11. Abdelkebir Khatibi, *Vomito Blanco: le sionisme et la conscience malheureuse* (Paris: Union générale d'édition, 1974), 7, 23, 47. Translation mine.

12. Mahmoud Darwich, *Pourquoi as-tu laissé le cheval à sa solitude?* (Paris: Actes Sud, 1996), 27–8. Translation mine.

13. A Jewish socialist movement created at the end of the 19th century in Poland and which opposes Zionism.

14. See Youssef Boussoumah's "Le sionisme expliqué à nos frères et à nos sœurs," Jun 2, 2014. https://www.youtube.com/watch?v=Xn2DFVj9Xc0.

15. Dieudonné, *Foxtrot*, 2012.

4. We, Indigenous Women

1. Translator's note: *beurette* is French slang for French woman whose family is originally North African (female version of the term "beur," which is verlan—ie: an inversion of syllables—for Arab)

2. I am a wall and the son of the people is a string.

3. I am a string and the son of the people is a wall.

4. Translator's note: *bwana* Arabic slang for boss (often used pejoratively).

5. Farida Belghoul, *Georgette!: Roman* (Paris: Éditions Bernard Barrault, 1986), 45–47. Translation mine.

6. Translator's note: Arabic term derived from the French word for workers, "les ouvriers" (which became "zouvriers"). Often used to refer to bachelors who came to work in Europe.

7. Translator's note: Ni Putes Ni Soumises is a French feminist movement and organization founded in 2003. See http://www.npns.fr/

8. Translator's note: *banlieusard* used to refer to someone living in the suburbs of a major city, especially Paris.

9. Translator's note: Dominique Strauss-Kahn.

10. Figures of reformism in Islam.

11. North African dialect used to refer to an Arab in a self-deprecating and humorous register.

12. Assata Shakur and Joanne Chesimard, "Women in Prison: How We Are," *The Black Scholar* (1978): 14.

13. See Tithi Bhattacharya, "Explaining gender violence in the neoliberal era," trans. Félix Boggio Éwanjé-Épée and Stella Magliani-Belkacem, *International Socialist Review* 91 (2013–2014). http://isreview.org/issue/91/explaining-gender-violence-neoliberal-era. Originally published as "Comprendre la violence sexiste à l'ère du néolibéralisme," *Revue Période*, http://revueperiode.net/comprendre-la-violence-sexiste-a-lere-du-neoliberalisme.

14. European feminism is of course plural. There are statist, liberal, neoliberal, imperialist or, on the contrary, radically, anti-liberal, anti-imperialist, and antiracist feminisms. Here, its dominant version is discussed.

15. Domenico Losurdo, *Le Péché originel du XXe siècle* (Brussels: Aden, 2007), 19, 21. Translation mine.

16. James Baldwin and Audre Lorde, "Revolutionary Hope: A Conversation Between James Baldwin and Audre Lorde," *Essence Magazine*, 1984, http://sonofbaldwin.tumblr.com/post/72976016835/triggerwarning-ableist-speech-sexismrevolutionary. All subsequent citations from Baldwin and Lorde are from this conversation.

17. See Oyèrónkẹ́ Oyěwùmí, *The Invention of Women: Making an African Sense of Western Gender Discourses* (Minneapolis: University of Minnesota Press, 1997).

18. Paola Bacchetta, "Réflexions sur les alliances feministes transnationales," in *Le Sexe de la mondialisation. Genre, class, race et nouvelle division du travail*, eds. Jules Falquet et al. (Paris: Les Presses de Sciences Po, 2010), 264–265.

19. Gordon Braxton, "This Sexual Assault Victim Didn't Report Her Rape Because She Wanted to Protect Me," *Huffington Post*, June 10, 2014, http://www.huffingtonpost.com/gordon-braxton/this-sexual-assault-victi_b_5125310.html?comm_ref=false&src=sp&utm_hp_ref=fb.

20. On the notion of sacrifice, see Houria Bouteldja, "Universalisme gay, homoracialisme, et 'mariage pour tous'" ["Gay Universalism, Homoracialism, and 'Marriage for All'"], *Parti des indigènes de la Républiques*, February 12, 2013, http://indigenes-republique.fr/universalisme-gay-homoracialisme-et-mariage-pour-tous-2/

5. We, Indigenous People

1. Translator's note: a *fellah* is a farmer or agricultural laborer in the Middle East and North Africa.

2. Translator's note: a *douar* is an Arabian village consisting typically of a group of tents or huts that encircle an open space.

3. El Ghalia, "Ya tayyra tiri biya," translation mine.

4. Noura, "Manich menna," translation mine.

5. Zaidi el Batni, "Ya Franca, ya Franca," translation mine.

6. Translator's note: the Companies Républicaines de Sécurité (CRS) are the general reserve of the French National Police.

7. El Mazouni, "Nakoul et khobz ou el ma," translation mine.

8. Translator's note: *bicot* is a pejorative and racist term used to refer to someone from North Africa.

9. El Mazouni, "Rani Jay," translation mine.

10. The "colonized's racism" (le "racisme édenté") is a term coined by Albert Memmi in *The Colonizer and the Colonized*, trans. Howard Greenfield (Boston: Beach Press, 1965), 175, originally published as *Portrait du Colonisé précédé du Portrait du Colonisateur* (Paris: Éditions Buchet/Chastel, 1957).

11. Translator's note: *cités de transit* were adopted in the 1970s as a means of rehousing Algerian families from cleared *bidonvilles* (or slum housing) during the construction of housing projects.

12. Khiari, *La contre-révolution coloniale en France*, 108–109. Translation mine.

13. Khiari, *La contre-révolution coloniale en France*, 206.

14. Belghoul, *Georgette!*, 162–3. Translation mine.

15. "'Black Power' Statement by the National Committee of Negro Churchmen, July 31, 1966," in Milton C. Sernett, *African American Religious History: A Documentary Witness* (Durham, NC: Duke University Press, 199), 556. Originally published in the *New York Times* (July 31, 1966).

16. Ramón Grosfoguel, "Decolonizing Post-Colonial Studies and Paradigms of Political Economy: Transmodernity, Decolonial Thinking and Global Coloniality," *Transmodernity: Journal of Peripheral Cultural Production of the Luso-Hispanic World*, 1 (2011), 1–37.

17. Translator's note: the *code de l'indigénat* was a set of laws creating an inferior legal status for natives of French colonies from 1887 to 1944–47, implemented first in Algeria and then applied throughout the French Colonial Empire from 1887 to 1889.

18. Aimé Césaire, "Culture and Colonization," trans. Brent Hayes Edwards, *Social Text* 103, 28 (2010): 139.

19. Jean Genet, Introduction to *Soledad Brother: The Prison Letters of George Jackson*, trans. Richard Howard (New York: Coward-McCann, Inc., 1970), n.p.

20. Sernett, African *American Religious History: A Documentary Witness*, 556.

21. Fatima Ouassak. "Nos parents immigré-e-s, une communauté des destin," *L'indigène de la République* (2006), 6. Translation mine.

22. The first Prime Minister of the Republic of China, who came into power in 1949 under Mao Zedong.

6. Allahou Akbar!

1. A hadith told by Muslim.

2. "… and Mohammed is his prophet" (declaration of faith in Islam).

3. René Viviani. Translation mine. http://www.museedeseineport. info/MuseeVirtuel/Salles/Viviani/Viviani.htm

4. Translator's note: a not-for-profit, charitable organization founded in 1985 by the comedian and actor Coluche.

5. Ashis Nandy, quoted in Guy Sorman, *Les Vrais penseurs de notre temps* (Paris: Fayard, 1989). Translation mine. http://www.philo5.com/ Les%20vrais%20penseurs/22%20-%20Ashis%20Nandy.htm

6. Ashis Nandy, preface to *The Intimate Enemy: Loss and Recovery of Self under Colonialism* (Delhi: Oxford University Press, 1983), ix–x.

7. God willing.

8. Dan Katchongva, "Hopi: A Message for All People. A Letter to the President of the United States of America," August 4, 1970, http://descendantofgods.tripod.com/id151.html.

9. James Baldwin, *The Fire Next Time* (New York: Vintage International, 1993), 105.

10. John Howard Griffin, *Black Like Me* (New York: Penguin, 2010), 98.

11. A bread made with semolina.

semiotext(e) intervention series
